Management for Professionals

The Springer series "Management for Professionals" comprises high-level business and management books for executives, MBA students, and practice-oriented business researchers. The topics cover all themes relevant to businesses and the business ecosystem. The authors are experienced business professionals and renowned professors who combine scientific backgrounds, best practices, and entrepreneurial vision to provide powerful insights into achieving business excellence.

The Series is SCOPUS-indexed.

Marc Vathauer

Breaking Barriers with Open Innovation in Germany

A Roadmap to Future-Proof Innovation for the Mittelstand

Springer

Marc Vathauer
MSF-Vathauer Antriebstechnik
Detmold, Germany

ISSN 2192-8096 ISSN 2192-810X (electronic)
Management for Professionals
ISBN 978-3-032-14659-5 ISBN 978-3-032-14660-1 (eBook)
https://doi.org/10.1007/978-3-032-14660-1

This Springer imprint is published by the registered company Springer Nature Switzerland AG
The registered company address is: Gewerbestrasse 11, 6330 Cham, Switzerland

I dedicate this book to everyone who contributed to its success with their knowledge, experience, and open minds. I would like to express my special thanks to all the experts, entrepreneurs, and researchers who shared their insights on open innovation in small and medium-sized enterprises with me.
My deepest gratitude goes to my family: My parents Inge und Karl-Ernst, who have always guided me with care and wisdom; my wife Tina and my son Niklas, who tirelessly gives me support, inspiration, and love; and all my relatives, who have supported and encouraged me during this intense period. Without your support, input, and patience, this work would not have been possible. This book is an expression of our shared journey towards greater openness, innovation, and growth.

Preface

Small and medium-sized enterprises (SMEs) face enormous challenges today: increasing competitive pressure, more complex markets, and shorter innovation cycles require continuous innovation. At the same time, many SMEs often lack the necessary resources to cover innovation processes entirely in-house. This is where the open innovation approach offers a valuable solution. By specifically involving external partners, networks, and knowledge sources, SMEs can significantly increase their innovation potential and respond more flexibly to market changes.

Open innovation makes it possible to overcome the limitations of traditional innovation models, compensate for knowledge and resource deficits, and jointly create more market-oriented, customer-focused innovations. Despite these opportunities, SMEs still face hurdles—such as the fear of knowledge loss, limited capacities, and the challenge of finding suitable partners. But it is precisely the ability to innovate that ensures the long-term competitiveness and viability of SMEs.

This book provides insights on how SMEs can use and implement the open innovation approach. It also provides insights of innovation activities of seven different industries beginning at the Automotive Industry till the Software- and Computer Service industry. Additionally, this book presents also a new possibility for a reimagined crowdsourcing platform for SMEs in order to use the crowdsourcing paradigm which has to be designed for SMEs requirements. It is aimed at anyone who has recognized the need for change and wants to take advantage of the opportunities offered by a networked innovation culture.

Detmold, Germany | Dr. Marc Vathauer

Competing Interests The author has no competing interests to declare that are relevant to the content of this manuscript.

Ethics Approval This book is based on the research conducted for the author's dissertation at the University of Portsmouth. The research involved a mixed-method approach, consisting of in-depth interviews and online surveys of predefined target groups. The author involves his professional network, by involving business partner such as supplier, customers, and innovation partner. Furthermore, some interim results have been pilot tested in the Author's own company, which is actually a traditional German manufacturing SME as mentioned below. In order to get information from the participants for his research project in order to be graduate with the Doctor of Business Administration from the University of Portsmouth, the Author has informed the interviewees upfront in writing about the uses of the research and the beneficial impact of it for German manufacturing SMEs. All conducted interviews were performed based on a signed agreement. The author of this book will commit to maintain confidentiality through his signature. All information has been treated with confidentiality and anonymously at all places. All social and cultural differences have been highly respected and treated equally by the author. Furthermore, all rights and interests of the author's participants have been protected and respected. Before an interview has been conducted, the respondent will be informed orally and in writing about the background of the research project and about the interviewer's profession. The author has informed the interviewees that all answers are voluntary, so that they may refuse to answer the question if the answer reveals corporate strategies or includes any strategic information.

Within the contacting phase, the potential participant has been informed about the purpose of the study (research), the aim (content), main aspects of the interview according to the prepared interview guideline and the reason for the choice of this person. Before the interview was started, the respondent was (again) informed about the ethical aspects of this research and their voluntary participation, the measures to ensure confidentiality and anonymity of the data and the opportunity to withdraw from participation and prevent the use of given information by the researcher at any time. In addition, he or she will be asked for consent to record the interview via digital recorder.

About the Book

This book addresses the pressing challenges facing small and medium-sized enterprises (SMEs) in today's rapidly evolving markets, where increasing competition, complexity, and shorter innovation cycles demand continuous innovation. Given that many SMEs lack sufficient internal resources to manage innovation on their own, the book presents the open innovation approach as a powerful solution. By engaging external partners, networks, and knowledge sources, SMEs can expand their innovation capabilities and adapt more flexibly to market changes.

The book explains how open innovation overcomes the limitations of traditional innovation by compensating for gaps in resources and knowledge and enabling the creation of customer-oriented, market-relevant innovations. Despite numerous opportunities, SMEs also face challenges such as fear of knowledge loss, limited capacities, and partner selection. However, innovation capability remains crucial to their long-term competitiveness and survival.

This book offers practical insights and proposes a novel crowdsourcing platform tailored to the needs of SMEs. It is essential reading for anyone who leads or runs a company and wants to actively shape innovation in his company.

This book examines the challenges and opportunities faced by German small and medium-sized enterprises (SMEs) in fostering innovation within an increasingly complex economic and technological environment. Drawing upon the dual perspective of Dr. Marc Vathauer—as both Managing Director of a traditional SME 'MSF-Vathauer Antriebstechnik (www.msf-technik.de)' and a researcher on open innovation—this work integrates practical managerial insights with academic inquiry. The book contextualizes German SMEs' innovation activities against recent economic developments, including the COVID-19 pandemic and projected stagnation in economic growth, emphasizing their vital contribution to Germany's trade surplus, employment levels, and international competitiveness. Despite their historical success, German SMEs encounter significant innovation barriers, such as talent shortages, high operating costs, insufficient digital infrastructure, financing constraints, and a lack of structured innovation management practices.

To address these challenges, the book employs a mixed-methods research design, combining qualitative interviews with SME leaders and a quantitative survey of 45,609 German SMEs. It evaluates the applicability of the open innovation paradigm—traditionally employed by multinational enterprises—to SMEs, highlighting its potential for enhancing competitiveness through structured innovation processes and strategic collaboration with external partners. Special attention is given to the role of innovation ecosystems, crowdsourcing platforms, and forecasting methods as tools for overcoming systemic barriers to innovation. The author proposes a novel crowdsourcing platform tailored to SMEs' specific needs, offering features that enable efficient partner identification, idea generation, and technology commercialization. By bridging theoretical research with practice-based insights, this book demonstrates how German SMEs can systematically leverage open innovation strategies to sustain their innovative capacity and secure long-term growth in a volatile global market.

Contents

About the Author

Dr. Marc Vathauer studied business administration and graduated with a master's degree. After completing his studies, he worked for a multinational enterprise in the automotive industry for several years before joining the family business MSF-Vathauer Antriebstechnik (www.msf-technik.de) in 2006, a German-based SME, specializes in drive technology and automation solutions. Additionally the company also offers customer-specific electronics solutions as well as comprehensive development and production services. Since then, in addition to his role as managing director, he has led various innovation projects and initiated international and national collaborations.

In parallel to his duties as Managing Director, he completed his doctorate at the University of Portsmouth on the topic of open innovation in German SMEs, which led the Doctor of Business Administration (DBA). Since then, Dr. Marc Vathauer has led several research and development projects in the context of innovation and has given presentations and lectures in his field of expertise.

Abbreviations

A.I.	Automotive Industry
AI	Artificial Intelligence
B	B is a regression coefficient and represents the slope of the line between the predictor variable and the dependent variable
B.V.	Besloten vennootschap met beperkte aansprakelijkheid (Dutch limited liability company)
BMBF	Bundesministerium für Bildung und Forschung (Englisch: Federal Ministry of Education and Research)
BMWi	Das Bundesministerium für Wirtschaft und Energie (English: Federal Ministry for Economic Affairs and Energy)
CEO	Chef Executive Officer
CIP	Continuous Improvement Process
CS	Cisco Systems
CTX	Citrix
Df	Degree of freedom
DIN EN ISO	DIN stands for German Institute for Standardization, EN for European Standard and ISO for International Organization for Standardization)
Dr.	Doktor
e. V.	Eingetragener Verein (English: Registered association)
EI	Electrical Industry
Et. Al	et alia
Etc.	Et cetera
EU	European Union
F	The F value is a value on the F distribution. Various statistical tests generate an F value. The value can be used to determine whether the test is statistically significant. The F value is used in analysis of variance (ANOVA). It is calculated by dividing two mean squares
GDP	Gross Domestic Product
GDPR	General Data Protection Regulation

GE	General Electric
GfK Enigma	German Market Research Institute
GmbH	Gesellschaft mit beschränkter Haftung (English: Ltd.)
GmbH & Co. KG	limited liability company & limited partnership
Hg.	Herausgeber (English: Editor)
HGB	German Accepted Accounting Principles
HI	Healthcare Industry
IBM	International Business Machines Corporation
ICT	Information and Communication Technology
Idw	Institute of Public Auditors in Germany
IfM	Institut für Mittelstandsforschung (English: Institute for SME Research)
IoT	Internet of Things
IIOT	Industrial Internet of Things
IP	Intellectual Property
IPR	Intellectual Property Rights
ISO	International Organization for Standardization
J	Japan
KPI	Key Performance Indicator
KVP	Kontinuierlicher Verbesserung Prozess (English: Continuous Improvement Process)
M&A	Mergers & Acquisitions
MD	Managing Director
MF	Manufacturing Industry
MI	Mechanical Industry
MID	Moulded Injection Design
MNC	Multinational Company
N.A.	Not Applicable
NDA	Non-Disclosure Agreement
NPD	New Product Development
NPV	Net Present Value
NRI	Network Readiness Index
OECD	Organisation for Economic Co-operation and Development
OEM	Original Equipment Manufacturer
OI	Open Innovation
p.	Page
p	p-value (probability value)
pp.	Pages
PCT	Patent Cooperation Treaty
PEMM	Process Enterprise Maturity Model
PTKA	Projektträger Karlsruhe (English: Promoter Karlsruhe)
PwC	PricewaterhouseCoopers (PricewaterhouseCoopers International is a global network of legally independent and independent companies in the areas of auditing, tax consultancy and business and management consulting)

QMS	Quality Management System
R	R—Linear Regression
R Square	R-squared is a goodness-of-fit measure for linear regression models. R-squared is a statistical measure of how close the data are to the fitted regression line
R&D	Research & Development
SANP	Supplier as no partner
SAP	Supplier as a partner
SCS	Software and Computer services Industry
Sig.	Significance
SME	Small and medium-sized enterprise
SO-Strategy	Strength and Opportunities-Strategy
SPSS	SPSS is a trademark of the software company IBM
Std. Error	Standard Error
STEM	Science, Technology, Engineering, and Mathematics
SWOT	Acronym for Strengths, Weaknesses, Opportunities and Threats analysis
t	t-value is a regression coefficient and determine whether to reject the null hypothesis
TPP	Target Product Profile
TQM	Total Quality Management
UK	United Kingdom
US	United States
USA	United States of America
VCI	Verband der Chemischen Industrie (English: Association of the Chemical Industry)
VDMA	Verband Deutscher Maschinen- und Anlagenbau (English: Mechanical Engineering Industry Association)
VR	Virtual Reality
WT-Strategy	Weaknesses and Threat-Strategy
ZVEI	Zentralverband Elektrotechnik- und Elektronikindustrie (English: German Electrical and Electronic Manufacturers' Association)

List of Figures

List of Tables

1 Introduction: Rationale, Motivation and Innovation Necessity in Small and Medium-Sized Enterprises

This book of innovation activities in German SMEs is motivated by personal experience of Dr. Marc Vathauer as an owner and Managing Director (MD) of the traditional SME MSF-Vathauer Antriebstechnik (www.msf-technik.de) in Germany, which he runs in the second Generation since 2006. The company is developing, producing and distributing decentralized drive technology, automation technology and electronic components for a wide range of industrial applications in the areas of Railway Technology, Environment Technology, Distribution and Logistic Technology (Warehouse and Intralogistics), Industrial Internet of Things (IIoT), Condition Monitoring and Predictive Maintenance systems. The company has initiated numerous government-funded R&D projects with external partners to develop new technologies and products. During this process, Dr. Marc Vathauer has realized the vital importance of identification of suitable R&D partners to work with as well as that of recognizing market developments and customer requirements. To anticipate future market developments, his company has used technological forecasting methods as well as the preference analysis (conjoint analysis) and many more. For the development of new technologies and products, the use of appropriate methods is necessary. However, also required is that the company work with appropriate external partners such as research institutes, universities and industrial organizations. Further, they developed new technologies and products that need to be successfully marketed in the corresponding markets. In this book, Dr. Marc Vathauer describes how traditional SMEs can become more innovative by employing certain methods from the overall open innovation approach. He draws his insights from his experience as a managing director and shareholder, as well as from his dissertation at the University of Portsmouth on the topic of open innovation in German SMEs.

The German economy—both large corporations and SMEs—experienced moderate to low economic growth in recent years following the coronavirus pandemic

M. Vathauer, *Breaking Barriers with Open Innovation in Germany*, Management for Professionals, https://doi.org/10.1007/978-3-032-14660-1_1

from 2020 to 2022 and the economic years 2023 to 2024. Some companies, particularly small and medium-sized enterprises, recorded losses, some of which resulted in their disappearance. The German Government predicts and slightly moderate economic growth of 0,3% for 2025 (Bundesministerium für Wirtschaft und Energie, 2025), whereas they have counted an economic deficit by minus 10% in 2020 and around zero per cent by 2022 (Bundesministerium für Wirtschaft und Energie 01.10.2022).

The former economic success of the German economy up until the onset of the COVID-19 pandemic led to a high trade surplus, a low unemployment rate and a high export rate in European and international comparison. German SMEs made a significant contribution to this economic growth prior to the pandemic between 2020 and 2023. This contribution is due to the own economic success of German SMEs, which in turn is due to their high innovative strength. It is important to build on the success of recent years in order to strengthen the innovativeness of the companies, maintain job opportunities and increase the resilience of companies against external and internal influences.

The term 'innovation' can be defined in different ways. The OECD (OECD, 2005, p. 46) defines innovation as '...the implementation of a new or significantly improved product (good or service), or process, a new marketing method, or a new organisational method in business practices, workplace organisation or external relations'. This definition comes from the so-called Oslo Manual, which serves as an internationally recognized guideline for measuring and classifying innovations (Schiefer, 2018). Chesbrough (Henry William Chesbrough, 2006, 2007; Timur & Antanas, 2017) defines innovation as '... creation of new wealth-producing resources or the endowment of existing resources with an enhanced potential for creating wealth, or creating products or services with an added value'. German SMEs, however, do not have a smooth path to innovation and they do face obstacles and difficulties in maintaining their economic success which hinder their ability to innovate and compete with international businesses. These include difficulties in recruiting skilled workers, high taxes, high energy costs, unfavourable climate for the digitization and problems in financing of their innovations. This is compounded by the fact that many of them do not follow a structured innovation management approach. Given this unfavourable external environment compounded by their own limitations how German SMEs can enhance their competitiveness against domestic and international businesses is the question that this book attempts to answer. For this, it first explores the causes of the previous success of the German economy and the related role of the innovativeness of German SMEs. It then examines the prospects of German economy and gives a brief insight into the likely obstacles and difficulties that German SMEs may face in future. To answer the specific question how German SME can improve their innovativeness, the book evaluates the results of a two-step data collection approach (mixed-method approach) was chosen in order to collect insights from German SME owner, Managing Directors and person who deploy in a leading position. It involved qualitative data collection by semi-structured in-depth interviews and a quantitative online survey of 45,609 German SMEs. Based on the findings of these interviews and survey, this book presents the wherewithal for the German SMEs to perform innovation in a structured manner to overcome the above-mentioned obstacles through the open innovation approach. This innovation approach is generally used by multinational enterprises that utilize their own open innovation ecosystems. This book summarizes the innovation ecosystems of well-known brands. It describes the innovation tools and the measures that the corporations use to perform their individual open innovation activities. Later, the book recommends the crowdsourcing platform and its design, functionalities and options as one particular innovation tool which German SMEs can use to pursue open innovation to perform their innovation activities in a structured manner and to maintain their innovativeness. It should be noted that crowdsourcing, as a part of the overall open innovation approach, is not a new tool in innovation management. However, it is used more often by for multinational enterprises than by the SMEs. This is not due to the lack of SMEs interest in the crowdsourcing concept, but it may be due to the lack of knowledge about it. It may also be due to the inability of German SMEs to find suitable crowdsourcing platforms that cater to their individual needs for innovation. For this reason, the author recommends a new crowdsourcing platform structure along with a set of features and functions which stands out from all other available crowdsourcing platforms and which suits the specific needs of the German SMEs. The literature on innovation shows that though open innovation approach is not very new, it has become popular among SMEs. This is because SMEs have only recently started its use sporadically whereas the Multinational Companies have been using it extensively and for a long time. They follow structured innovation closely linked to an open innovation approach as shown in Table 1.1 and suggest that the open innovation approach is not suitable for SMEs, because it involves start-up integration, idea creation, funding and web-based innovation, which only large multinational companies can execute.

Multinational Enterprises follow a structured innovation process that must be strictly adhered to in order to achieve innovation success. Below are four examples of well-known large corporations illustrate how these companies innovate and what measures have been introduced in these companies.

1.1 General Electric (GE)

General Electric (GE) is trying to solve problems by so-called advanced manufacturing techniques. They are using crowdsourcing techniques across industries to improve its customer value. General Electric collaborates with experts and entrepreneurs such as customers or suppliers to get new insights, ideas and expertise. Furthermore they launch different initiatives for open innovation challenges and they invite the global community to provide ideas, new approaches, new technologies and technology proposals for specific topics and issues (General Electric, 2016). Additionally General Electric also launched an initiative called ‘FirstBuild’ which is an online and physical community for designing, engineering, building

Table 1.1 Overview of open innovation activities in multinational enterprises

			Innovation activities								
Companies	Country	Programme name	Crowdsourcing		Customer integration	Supplier integration	Intellectual Property Management	Entrepreneurs integration		Idea creation funding	
			Innovation challenges by Internet platform	Startup incubation / acceleration programme				Startup's	Idea exchange with settled companies	Direct	Venture Capital access
General Electric	US	FirstBuild	x		x	x	x	x	x	x	
Cisco Systems	US	Entrepreneurs in Residence		x				x			x
Samsung	J	Samsung Accelerator programme		x				x			x
Telefonica	ES	Wayra		x				x		x	
Citrix	US	Startup Accelerator		x	x			x			x
Microsoft	US	Microsoft Ventures Accelerators		x				x			
Shell	GB	Shell GameChanger programme	x					x	x	x	
Turner/ Warner Bos	US	Media Camp						x	x	x	

(continued)

Table 1.1 (continued)

			Innovation activities								
Companies	Country	Programme name	Crowdsourcing		Customer integration	Supplier integration	Intellectual Property Management	Entrepreneurs integration		Idea creation funding	
			Innovation challenges by Internet platform	Startup incubation / acceleration programme				Startup's	Idea exchange with settled companies	Direct	Venture Capital access
Google	US	Google for Entrepreneurs		x				x		N.A	N.A
Orange	ES	The Orange Fab		x			x	x			x

and selling new home appliances (Innovation Excellence, 2014). In addition to this Hutter, Hautz, Repke, Matzler (Hutter et al., 2013, p. 12) emphasize that a major number of multinational enterprises (60%–70%) are using web-based technologies to integrate external stakeholder such as customers and external experts.

1.2 Cisco Systems (CS)

Cisco Systems (CS) launched a start-up incubation programme 'Entrepreneurs in Residence' to provide a platform for strategic relationships with early-stage entrepreneurs in the USA and Europe. The focus of this programme is the knowledge creation by collaborative start-ups, which work on their own account but they have to provide their knowledge and new solutions to Cisco Systems. During the programme, 'Entrepreneurs in Residence' the start-ups can collaborate with other start-ups and they could build their own 'start-up family'. Additionally Cisco Systems provides several events for their start-ups such as networking events, or marketing and public relations opportunities, or legal support, or access to Venture Capital organizations (Cisco Systems Inc., 2016).

1.3 Citrix (CTX)

The accelerator programme from CITRIX is an open innovation platform, which develops and funds start-ups in Silicon Valley (USA), Santa Barbara (USA), and Bengaluru (India). The programme considers start-ups (early-stage entrepreneurial teams) which are coached by specialists from CITRIX and they train the leadership skills as well as the design thinking activities. They incorporate customer traction and they develop leadership. Hutter (Hutter et al., 2013) emphasize that customer integration is also the most frequently applied tool to operate open innovation in SMEs and in multinational enterprises. CITRIX works with several entrepreneurs which are funded by CITRIX due to a special Venture programme (CITRIX Startup Accelerator, 2014).

1.4 Shell (SH)

Contrary to all above described accelerator programmes, the company Shell provides a programme for private person and for external companies as well as for the entire Shell group, which is called 'Shell GameChanger'. Shell provides innovators around the world with financial and technical support to demonstrate technical and commercial viability of their ideas. Innovators are invited to submit their ideas onto an online website. After the validation of the ideas from a screening panel, the innovator must submit a proof-concept. After passing the proof-concept, a funding of the idea is possible by Shell. The innovator is encouraged to use such funding to develop the idea in accordance with the agreed plan by the panel experts (Shell International B.V., 2014).

As mentioned by the above shown cases, most of the multinational enterprises execute their open innovation activities by incorporated start-up companies which are supported by the enterprises financial or advisory wise. They launched start-up incubation programmes or innovation accelerator programmes around the world to get new ideas, new insights and new problem-solving approaches. Additionally, to this, some multinational enterprises incorporate also online platforms to get new insights from the public, the so-called crowdsourcing.

Keeping this in mind, this book addresses the necessity and proposes a specific 'Crowdsourcing' tool for open innovation by German SMEs to compensate for their resource inadequacy. Additionally, it also proposes the wherewithal for German SMEs to execute structured innovation.

References

Bundesministerium für Bildung und Forschung (BMBF). (2025). *Technologisch souverän in Deutschland und Europa*. Berlin.

Chesbrough, H. W. (2007). Why companies should have open business models. *MIT Sloan Management Review, 48*(2).

Chesbrough, H. W. (2006). *Open business models: How to thrive in the new innovation landscape*. Harvard Business School Press.

Cisco Systems Inc. (2016). *Entrepreneurs in residence*. https://eir.cisco.com/

CITRIX Startup Accelerator. (2014). *The startup accelerator is an open innovation platform that develops and funds startups and corporate internal teams*. http://startupaccelerator.vc/innovators-program/

General Electric. (2016). *GE open innovation*. http://www.ge.com/about-us/openinnovation

Hutter, K., Hautz, J., Repke, K., & Matzler, K. (2013). Open innovation in small and micro enterprises. *Problems and Perspectives in Management, 11*(1), 12–22.

Innovation Excellence. (2014). *15 Examples of open innovation between big companies & startups*. http://www.innovationexcellence.com/blog/2014/08/13/15-examples-of-open-innovation-between-big-companies-startups/

OECD. (2005). *The measurement of scientific and technological activities: Proposed guidelines for collecting and interpreting technological innovation data*. OECD Publishing.

Schiefer, A. (2018). Oslo manual 2018: Guidelines for collecting, reporting and using data on innovation, 4th edn. *Statistische Nachrichten*, 963–697.

Shell International B. V. (2014). *Shell GameChanger*. http://www.shell.com/energy-and-innovation/innovating-together/shell-gamechanger.html#vanity-aHR0cDovL3d3dy5zaGVsbC5jb20vZ2xvYmFsL2Z1dHVyZS1lbmVyZ3kvaW5ub3ZhdGlvbi9pbm5vdmF0ZS13aXRoLXNoZWxsL3NoZWxsLWdhbWVjaGFuZ2VyLmh0bWw

Timur, K., & Antanas, M. (2017). The definition and classification of innovation. *HOLISTICA, 8*(1), 59–72.

Innovation Activities in Small and in Large Companies

2

Different companies innovate differently. Some prefer a structured innovation approach and others prefer a more ad hoc approach. Due to the high degree of individuality, a generally valid statement cannot be made as to how a company adopts its innovation procedure. The chapter highlights some studies that show that the size of the company has an impact on innovation success and that larger companies have better innovation performance. However, it also reports some studies which show the opposite. This chapter also discusses Cooper's (Cooper, 2010) stage gate model as a structured way to perform innovation activities in the company.

There are different strengths and weaknesses of SMEs vis-à-vis large corporations when it comes to innovation. Many specific characteristics of SMEs' can be seen as their critical success factors for innovation. Many studies have analyzed the relationship between innovation and the size of the company. Recent research shows that the size of a company and innovation activity have a positive correlation which means that larger companies tend to be more innovative. It also shows that larger is the impact on performance of open innovation the larger the business is (de Jong & Vermeulen, 2014; Ebersberger et al., 2010; Eurostat-European Commission, 2013; Püchner et al., 2017; Schwarz et al., 2024; Sullivan & Kang, 1999). However, many other studies also report a negative correlation between the company's size and innovation (Damanpour, 1996; Grundström et al., 2012; Pianta & Vaona, 2006; Stock et al., 2002). Obviously, there is no consistency in the findings related to the link between these two variables. SMEs' biggest strengths—often mentioned—is that they can react to the environment fast and flexibly due to the fact that internal structures, procedures and organizational conditions are strongly shaped by the entrepreneurs themselves and often hierarchies are. However, due to very flexible structures and no formal communication, sometime in SMEs the communication can suffer and this leads to costly delays (Spielkamp & Rammer, 2006).

M. Vathauer, *Breaking Barriers with Open Innovation in Germany*, Management for Professionals, https://doi.org/10.1007/978-3-032-14660-1_2

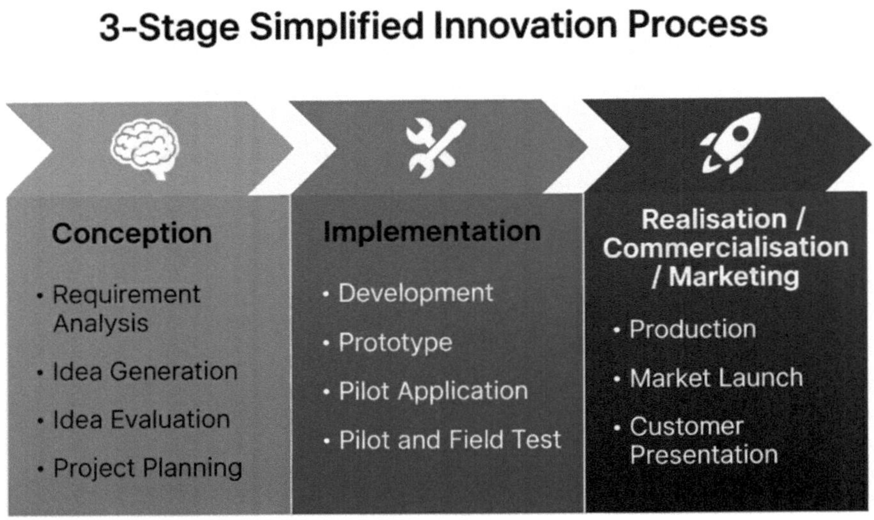

Fig. 2.1 3-Stage simplified innovation process; based on (Verworn & Herstatt, 2000, p. 3)

The innovation process at SMEs does not take place in a static environment. It is the result of a dynamic process. This process is influenced by internal factors such as employees, and management team and external factors linked to the customers supplier or competitors (Verworn et al., 2000, pp. 2–22). Innovations need a structured process involving systematic steps (Tiwari & Buse, 2007). These steps can be represented in a simple innovation process diagram in Fig. 2.1.

The Flow chart titled '3-Stage Simplified Innovation Process' with three stages shows the innovation process which is divided into discrete phases. After each phase, management reviews the progress and decides on the progression to the next phase. Thus, activities that were otherwise performed ad hoc are standardized. This ensures the completion of each task. However, this may also expose each stage to a go-no-go decision and thus the process is slowed (Verworn & Herstatt, 2000, pp. 4–11).

The innovation process shown above is based on Cooper's (Cooper, 2010) Stage-Gate Model which was developed in the 1960s and redeveloped in the 1980s. The Stage-Gate Model divides the innovation process into particular sections and follows an orderly sequence of task areas. The sections are referred to as 'stages'. After passing each stage through so-called checkpoints, the 'gates' have to be passed. The project is evaluated at each 'gate' and a decision-making process considers the termination or continuing of the project. The use of a 'game plan', a standardized approach to development projects, has been identified as a key success factor (Verworn & Herstatt, 2000, pp. 4–6). Thus, there is a normative model the application of which to increase the company's success is recommended.

The flowchart in Fig. 2.2 titled '5-Stage Innovation Review Process' illustrating the progression from 'IDEA' to 'REVIEW' in an innovation process and includes

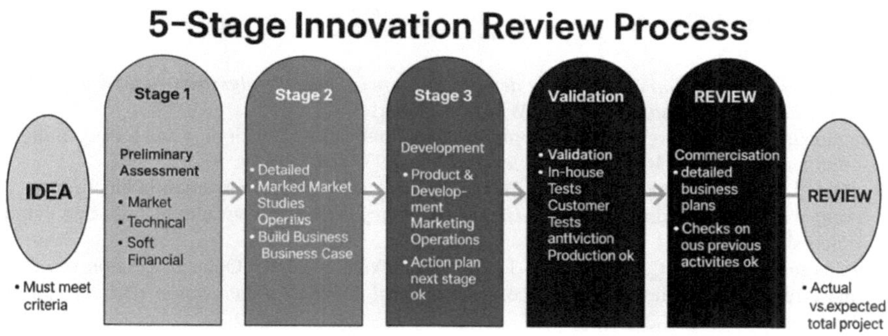

Fig. 2.2 5-Stage innovation review process; based on (Verworn & Herstatt, 2000, pp. 2–5)

all key managerial functions. The decisions at the 'gates' are taken across functions using defined 'go' or 'kill' criteria. The individual activities do not run strictly sequentially. Overlaps are possible and they speed up the process. The benefits of the introduction of a Stage-Gate process in practice are in the systematization of otherwise often ad hoc running development. The process is transparent, and a common understanding is developed. This facilitates both communication within the team and communication with top management (Verworn & Herstatt, 2000, p. 4). The Stage-Gate Model contains advantages to develop particular products or services in a 'closed shop' manner. In contrast, the open innovation approach requires companies, to open their boundaries, as mentioned earlier, and they have to let new ideas into the company from the outside.

2.1 Summary of the Chapter

As described at the beginning of this chapter, there is no evidence of an inherent link between the company size and its innovation success. Verworn et al. (2000, pp. 4–6, 12–13) emphasize that innovation activity in SMEs is the result of a dynamic process and is influenced by internal and external factors. The more structured innovation activities in larger companies follow more systematic steps (Tiwari & Buse, 2007) as represented by the Stage-Gate model. In this context, SMEs' biggest strength is that they can react quickly and flexibly towards customer's requirements and market changes due to their entrepreneurial nature whereas, larger companies tend to follow a more structured innovation approach. However, it is also true that due to too much flexibility and the informal communication the SMEs' innovation activities may suffer and lead to costly delays (Spielkamp & Rammer, 2006).

The next chapter analyzes the closed and open innovation approaches.

References

Cooper, R. G. (2010). *Top oder Flop in der Produktentwicklung: Erfolgsstrategien: Von der Idee zum Launch (Sonderausg* (2nd ed.). Wiley-VCH-Verl.

Damanpour, F. (1996). Organizational complexity and innovation: Developing and testing multiple contingency models. *Management Science, 42*(5), 693–716.

De Jong, J. P., & Vermeulen, P. A. (2014). Determinants of product innovation in small firms: A comparison across industries. *EIM business and policy research.* www.eim.nl/smes-and-entrepreneurship

Ebersberger, B., Bloch, C., Herstad, S. J., & van der Velde. (2010). Open innovation practices and effect on innovation performance. *International Journal of Innovation and Technology Management, 9*(6), 1–23.

Eurostat-European Commission. (2013). *Science, technology and innovation in Europe.* Luxembourg: Publications Office of the European Union, 2013. Advance online publication. https://doi.org/10.2785/35613

Grundstrüm, C., Sjöström, R., Uddenberg, A., & Rönnbäck, A. Ö. (2012). Fast-Growing SME's and the role of innovation. *International Journal of Innovation Management, 16*(03), 1240003. https://doi.org/10.1142/S1363919612400038

Pianta, M., & Vaona, A. (2006). Firm size and innovation in European manufacturing: Kiel Working Paper No. 1284. *The Kiel Institute for the World Economy*, 1–22.

Püchner, D. P., Fischer, H., & Schmidt, A. (2017). *Open innovation—Strategische Herangehensweisen für kleine und mittlere Unternehmen* (1st ed.). Stuttgart.

Schwarz, N., Finger, L., Burk, M., David, A., Gero, S., & Pascal, H. (2024). Open innovation in Unternehmen in Deutschland: Ergebnisse des open transfer index. *Stifterverband Für Die Deutsche Wissenschaft*, pp. 3–25. https://www.stifterverband.org/sites/default/files/2024-

Spielkamp, A., & Rammer, C. (2006). Balanceakt innovation Erfolgsfaktoren im innovationsmanagement kleiner und mittlerer Unternehmen. *Zentrum für Europäische Wirtschaftsforschung*, (06–04).

Stock, G. N., Greis, N. P., & Fischer, W. A. (2002). Firm size and dynamic technological innovation. *Technovation, 22*(9), 537–549. https://doi.org/10.1016/S0166-4972(01)00061-X

Sullivan, P., & Kang, J. (1999). Quick response adoption in the apparel manufacturing industry:Competitive advantage of innovation. *Journal of Small Business Management, 37*(1), 1–13.

Tiwari, R., & Buse, S. (2007). Barriers to innovation in SMEs: Can the internationalization of R&D mitigate their effects? *Working Papers/Technologie- Und Innovationsmanagement, Technische Universität Hamburg-Harburg, 50*, 1–31.

Verworn, B., & Herstatt, C. (2000). Modelle des Innovationsprozesses. *Working Papers/ Technologie- und Innovationsmanagement, Technische Universität Hamburg-Harburg, 6*, 1–15. http://nbn-resolving.de/urn:nbn:de:gbv:830-opus-1607

3 The Closed Innovation Versus Open Innovation

3.1 Introduction

Globalization and shortened product life cycles have put the SMEs as well as the multinational corporations under competitive pressures. They must continue to innovate to survive and grow. However, the resources needed for investments and other preliminary work for the implementation of innovations far exceed the capacity of small companies. For effective innovation management as well as for risk minimization, there is a need for work on innovation in conjunction with other providers, suppliers or customers. For innovation, two approaches are available to SMEs. The closed innovation approach and the open innovation approach. The principles of closed innovation can be summarized as follows. The organization tries to find and hire the innovation capable employees and tries to let research, development and marketing of an innovation take place internally. In closed innovation only the ideas from internal research can contribute to success, provided that they also outperform the competition. It ensures that the intellectual property does not reach the competitors. The open innovation concept, in contrast, provides for companies to open their boundaries to other actors and thus use external expertise for innovation activities. The extent of integration of open innovation in the business model varies in practice.

3.1.1 The Closed Innovation Approaches

The closed innovation approach describes the logic of closed innovation as one of closed, centralized, internal research and development (Henry William Chesbrough, 2006b, p. 29). At its roots, the logic implies a need for deep vertical integration. One must do everything internally. Outside the fortified central R&D castles, the knowledge landscape was assumed to be rather barren. Consequently,

M. Vathauer, *Breaking Barriers with Open Innovation in Germany*, Management for Professionals, https://doi.org/10.1007/978-3-032-14660-1_3

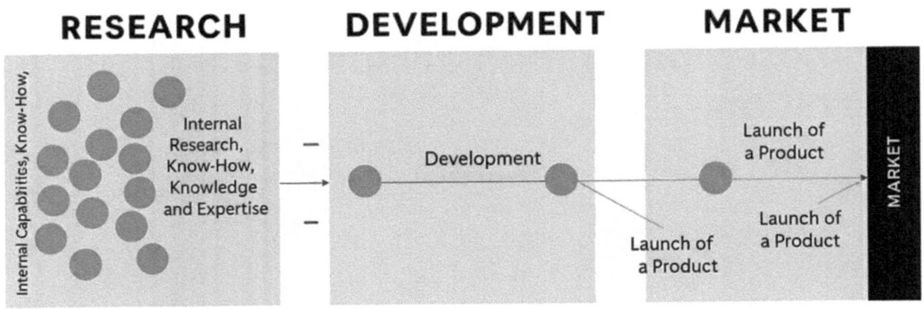

Fig. 3.1 The logic of closed innovation; based on (Henry William Chesbrough, 2006b, p. xxii)

the firm should rely on itself. The flowchart in Fig. 3.1 'The logic of closed innovation' illustrating the process from research to market and it shows the working of the closed innovation approach, underpinned by the closed boundaries of a company.

3.1.2 The Open Innovation Approach

Imagine a world where companies no longer guard their ideas like hidden treasures but instead open their doors to the outside world. That's the essence of Open Innovation. Open innovation is a mindset—a paradigm shift—that suggests companies should use not only their internal ideas and resources but also those from the outside (Henry William Chesbrough, 2006b, p. xxiv). Think of it as a two-way street: ideas flow in and out, and business models are built to turn all these ideas—regardless of where they come from—into value, which the flowchart in Fig. 3.2 'The logic of open innovation' is illustrating.

Over the past decade, open innovation has transformed how firms manage innovation (Bigliardi et al., 2020; Blümel, 2019; Fredberg, Elmquist, & Ollila,

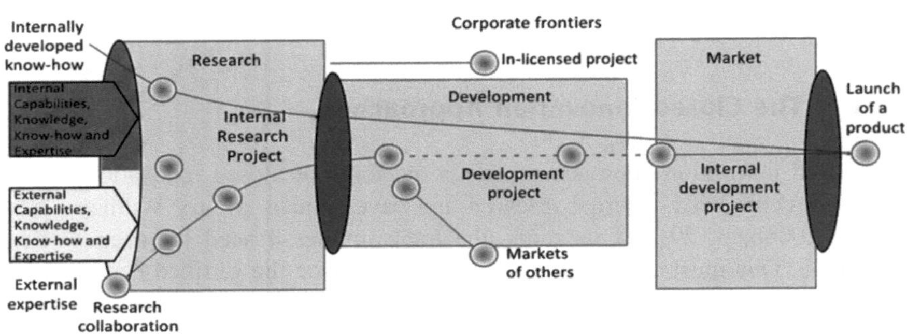

Fig. 3.2 The logic of open innovation; based on (Henry William Chesbrough, 2006b, p. xxv)

pp. 5–58; Gassmann et al., 2010, pp. 213–221; Gassmann & Sutter, 2013; Püchner et al., 2017; Vanhaverbeke et al., 2012, pp. 1–99; Welter & Woll, 2021).

The key idea is this: to innovate successfully, companies need to break down their walls. By tapping into both internal and external ideas, firms can speed up technological advancement and increase their chances of success in the market. Small and medium-sized enterprises (SMEs), for instance, often collaborate horizontally with customers and suppliers. (Verworn et al., 2000) or vertically with research institutions to develop breakthrough technologies (Parida et al., 2012, pp. 285–293). Research shows that SMEs team up with universities or R&D centres to gain fresh insights (Parida et al., 2012, pp. 285–291).

However, the integration of user (customer) into the open innovation approach is mostly beneficial due to their knowledge and the necessary expertise while companies innovate (Trott et al., 2013, p. 127). But not all customers are equally helpful. It's often the so-called *lead users*—those passionate tinkerers and early adopters—who drive the real innovations. Still, there's a key distinction: invention is not always innovation (Trott et al., 2013, p. 129).

Sometimes such approach flips, by partnerships and competitors foster incremental innovation, while ties with universities spur radical innovation. The catch? Radical innovation often needs a little extra push to become commercially viable—and that's where business creativity and effort come into play (Belderbos et al., 2004, pp. 1486–1490).

Collaborating with outside partners means being vulnerable. You're opening up your company's boundaries, which calls for an open mind (Rahman & Ramos, 2013, pp. 431–448). But it's worth it. Open innovation is a new way of thinking that helps firms profit from innovation. The firms once create value by new ideas and solutions and they capture value by turning those ideas into profit (Henry William Chesbrough, 2006a, p. 17; Reichwald & Möslein, 2010, pp. 1–15). Gassmann and Enkel (2004). They can process it in three different ways:

1. Outside-In: Bringing in knowledge and ideas from customers, suppliers, and research institutions to boost your company's own expertise.
2. Inside-Out: Sharing internal ideas and technologies with the outside world—often to find new markets or to sell/licence IP.
3. Coupled: A powerful mix of both, usually done in partnerships or alliances with complementary organizations.

The opening of the company's boundaries is beneficial on the one hand, but includes also risks on the other, even if the companies opening up parts of their value chain and even their intellectual property. Giving outsiders access to sensitive information means trusting that their intentions align with yours (Gassmann & Enkel, 2004, pp. 10–11).

3.2 Summary of the Chapter

The closed innovation approach is a more centralized approach where the companies perform their innovation activities internally rather than externally. They rely on themselves, try to do everything in-house and avoid involvement of any external agency. This behaviour results in longer time to market, intensive and costly development processes as R&D projects take long time to fruition. In addition, such firms miss to use the latest technologies developed elsewhere and end up developing non-competitive products. Contrary to this, companies following the open innovation approach open their company's boundaries to let new knowledge into the firm. Such firms open their processes and use a combination of the external and internal ideas, have better technology development and shorter times to market. Collaboration with others leads to incremental innovation as well as to radical innovation depending on the capabilities of the external R&D partner. The open innovation approach also enables companies to revamp their business model to enhance their market share or to find new business opportunities.

References

Belderbos, R., Carree, M., & Lokshin, B. (2004). Rahman. *Research Policy, 33*(10), 1477–1492. https://doi.org/10.1016/j.respol.2004.07.003

Bigliardi, B., Ferraro, G., Filippelli, S., & Galati, F. (2020). The influence of open innovation on firm performance. *International Journal of Engineering / Business Management*, 1–14.

Blümel, C. (2019, September 5). *Open science und open innovation: Neue Indikatoren für die Analyse des Wissenschaftsund Innovationssystems im digitalen Zeitalter* (No. 1). Essen. Retrieved from Stifterverband für die Deutsche Wissenschaft e.V website: file:///C:/Users/Marc.Vathauer/Downloads/open_science_und_open_innovation_discussion_paper.pdf

Chesbrough, H. W. (2006a). *Open business models: How to thrive in the new innovation landscape*. Harvard Business School Press.

Chesbrough, H. W. (2006b). *Open innovation: The new imperative for creating and profiting from technology*. Harvard Business School Press.

Gassmann, O., & Enkel, E. (2004). *Towards a theory of open innovation: Three core process archetypes: Towards a theory of open innovation: Three core process archetypes,* 1–18. https://www.alexandria.unisg.ch/publications/274

Gassmann, O., & Sutter, P. (2013). *Praxiswissen Innovationsmanagement: Von der Idee zum Markterfolg* (3., überarb.und erw. Aufl). Hanser.

Gassmann, O., Enkel, E., & Chesbrough, H. W. (2010). The future of open innovation. *R&D Management, 40*(3), 213–221.

Parida, V., Westerberg, M., & Frishammar, J. (2012). Inbound open innovation activities in high-tech SMEs: The impact on innovation performance. *Journal of Small Business Management, 50*(2), 283–309.

Püchner, D. P., Fischer, H., & Schmidt, A. (2017). *Open innovation—Strategische Herangehensweisen für kleine und mittlere Unternehmen* (1st ed.). Stuttgart.

Rahman, H., & Ramos, I. (2013). Challenges in adopting open innovation strategies in SMEs: An exploratory study in Portugal. *Issues in Informing Science and Information Technology., 10*, 431–448.

Reichwald, R., & Möslein, K. M. (2010). Management offener Innovationsprozesse. *CLIC—Center for Leading Innovation & Cooperation, 19*, 1–15.

Trott, P., van der Duin, P., & Hartmann, D. (2013). Users as innovators? Exploring the limitations of user-driven innovation. *Prometheus, 31*(2), 125–138. https://doi.org/10.1080/08109028.2013.818790

Vanhaverbeke, W., Mermeersch, I., & de Zutter, S. (2012). Open Inovation in SMEs: How can small companies and start-ups benefit from open innovation stragegies? *ResearchReport, Vlerick Leuven Gent Management School, März,* 1–99.

Verworn, B., Lüthje, C., & Herstatt, C. (2000). Innovationsmanagement in kleinen und mittleren Unternehmen. *Working Papers/Technologie- und Innovationsmanagement, Technische Universität Hamburg-Harburg, 7.*

Welter, F., & Woll, C. (Eds.). (2021). *Handbuch KMU-Management: Grundlagen, Strategien und Praxisbeispiele.* Springer Gabler.

4 Opportunities for and Challenges to the Success of German Small and Medium-Sized Enterprises

4.1 Introduction

This chapter and the following sub-chapters deal with the opportunities and challenges associated with the business success of German SMEs. The success of the German economy and its structure with regard to the most important sectors, the types of companies and their number of employees as well as the current themes of Industry 4.0 and digitization and the digitalization are discussed. Furthermore, the necessity, the importance as well as the need for supporting the German SMEs for the overall success of the economy are discussed, underpinned by the statistical evidence. In addition, drivers for German economic success are discussed using the economic structure and their importance for the overall system. Statistical data is used to discuss the current standing of German innovation capability in European comparison, competitiveness in a global comparison and the digitization prospects in comparison to other economies. Based on these findings, innovation challenges for German SMEs are explicated that make it difficult for companies to be innovative and to keep up with national and global competition. Based on these, open innovation is a possible innovation approach, which enables multinational companies as well as SMEs to innovate and thus withstand the increasing competitive pressure.

4.2 The German Economy Is Treading Water and the Role of Small and Medium-Sized Enterprises

SMEs are identified by two measures: the size of a company and the economic nature of the entity. The §267 HGB (German GAAP) (Federal Ministry of Justice and Consumer Protection, 2015) distinguishes SMEs according to its characteristics, as shown in Table 4.1. As inflation affects the monetary variables, such as

M. Vathauer, *Breaking Barriers with Open Innovation in Germany*, Management for Professionals, https://doi.org/10.1007/978-3-032-14660-1_4

Table 4.1 Size-related definition of Small and medium-sized enterprises

Size of Enterprise	Number of Employees		Total assets		Turnover € / Year
Small	<=50	and	<=6 Mio €	or	<=12 Mio €
Mid-Sized	<=250	and	<=20 Mio €	or	<=40 Mio €
Big companies	>250	and	>20 Mio €	or	>40 Mio €

source (Federal Ministry of Justice and Consumer Protection, 2015)

sales for the empirical field study, the number of employees remains a useful and pragmatic delimitation feature.

A key contributor to the economic success of German SMEs is that most of them have positioned themselves into niche providers in their industries to counteract and compensate for the above-mentioned competitive pressures. A large number of German SMEs offer individual, customer-specific solutions or even niche solutions. On the back of this business strategy, some German SMEs have become world market leaders in their industry and are called 'Hidden Champions' (Simon, 2007, p. 16). Another factor that has contributed to the economic success of SMEs is that they try to keep their employees employed even in difficult economic times as shown during the financial crisis in 2008 and during the COVID-19 pandemic, unlike multinational companies. As it is increasingly difficult for SMEs to recruit well-educated employees, this strategy is another success factor in retaining their competitiveness. Traditional SMEs are also mostly rooted within the regions in which they are located and its owners are committed to the region and also focused on a possible expansion of the company in the same location. Another of their strength is that they can react much faster than multinational enterprises to changing customer requirements or market changes. However, these advantages of SMEs are getting offset by huge market penetration, market presence and greater product acceptance of multinational companies.

Generally the German economy has faced notable challenges and moderate growth fluctuations in recent years. After contracting by 0.3% in 2023 and a further 0.2% in 2024, the economy showed signs of recovery in early 2025, with GDP rising by 0.4% in the first quarter compared to the previous quarter (Statistisches Bundesamt, 2025b, 2025d). Employment has remained relatively stable, with the number of employed persons hovering around 46 million and the unemployment rate expected to be about 6.2% in 2025 (Wollmershäuser, 2025). In this context, it must be mentioned Germany recorded the highest number of corporate insolvencies in about ten years. According to the Federal Statistical Office and Creditreform, approximately 12,000 corporate insolvencies were registered in the first half of 2025—an increase of approximately 12% compared to the same period in 2024 (approximately 10,880 cases) (Institut für Mittelstandsforschung Bonn; Statistisches Bundesamt, 2025c; Verband der Vereine Creditreform e. V., 2025).

Table 4.2 R&D to sales ratio in key German industries in 2023

Industry	Turnover 2023	Investments into innovations	R&D to sales ratio[1]
Automotive	€420.00 billion	€51.00 billion	12.1%
Mechanical Engineering	€265.00 billion	€17.00 billion	6.4%
Chemical industry	€202.00 billion	€8.40 billion	4.2%
Pharmaceutical industry	€54.00 billion	€12.20 billion	22.6
Food industry	€185.00 billion	€2.25 billion	1.2%
Electrical industry	€192.00 billion	€9.00 billion	4.7%

source (Statista GmbH, 2025d)

Nevertheless, SMEs continue to play a crucial role in the German economy, accounting for roughly one-third of total GDP—a share that has remained consistent through 2025. Although Germany is no longer the fastest-growing economy in the EU, it maintains a reputation for resilience and stability. The country's economic strength is still largely attributed to its high export volumes, underpinned by the global reputation of German engineering, product quality, and the durability of its goods. Germany remains the EU's leading export nation, followed by the Netherlands, France, Italy, and Spain. In 2024, the value of Germany's exported goods was approximately €1562 billion, while imports amounted to €1370 billion, resulting in a trade surplus of about €192 billion (Wollmershäuser, 2025). Key industries with the highest R&D intensity—such as automotive, machinery, chemicals, and electronics—continue to drive this export performance. For 2025, the German manufacturing sector is projected to generate revenues of roughly €1950 billion, reflecting its ongoing significance as a major contributor to GDP and exports. German manufacturing firms continue to invest a substantial share of their turnover in innovation and R&D to maintain competitiveness and support export growth. Despite ongoing structural challenges—such as high energy costs, skilled labour shortages, and increased global competition—the German economy is expected to gradually return to more robust growth from 2026 onward, provided that domestic and international conditions stabilize (Deutsche Bundesbank, 2025; Wollmershäuser, 2025). Such figures were driven by six key German industries with highest R&D rate as shown in Table 4.2. Its manufacturing companies invest a large part of their turnover into innovation to generate such turnover and to maintain their competitiveness (Statista GmbH, 2025d).

In addition to high R&D turnover ratios in Germany's most important industrial sectors, the unemployment rate is at a medium level, although it has increased in recent years. After declining from 11.7% in 2005 to 5.2% in 2018, the unemployment rate increased to an average of 5.7% in 2023 and reached 6.2% in May 2025, the highest level since 2020 (Statista GmbH, 2025a, 2025e). While

[1] The relationship between ,Investments into innovations by industry and, 'industry turnover 2023'

Table 4.3 Number of companies, Size versus legal forms

	0–9 Employees	10–49 Employees	50–249 Employees	More than 249 Employees	TOTAL
Individual entrepreneurs	1,954,811	89,627	3540	85	2,048,063
Partnerships (e.g. OHG, KG)	335,851	64,122	14,322	3231	417,526
Corporations (GmbH, AG)	591,177	181,460	49,919	11,334	833,890
Other legal forms	132,816	27,618	7328	2677	170,439
TOTAL	3,014,655	362,827	75,109	17,327	3,469,918

source (Statista GmbH, 2025f)

a low unemployment rate benefits job seekers, it presents challenges for businesses—especially SMEs—as it becomes increasingly difficult to find suitable employees. This shortage has continued to drive up wages, first among skilled workers and subsequently among unskilled workers. The economic growth outlined above has been possible due to the diversity of the German economy, which comprised approximately 3.5 million companies across Germany in 2024, as shown in Table 4.3.

These companies employed around 30.5 million people with social insurance, generating a total sales turnover of about €6800 billion in 2024, of which SMEs accounted for roughly €2400 billion (about 35% of GDP) (IfM Bonn, 2025; Vergabeblog.de, 2024). The strong manufacturing value chain within Germany is a key driver of economic growth, as the services sector alone contributes less due to limited value creation. However, German SMEs and multinational enterprises now face significant challenges, including rising international competition from low-cost producers in emerging markets and the need to respond through greater automation or new business models. Additionally, the digitalization of production and the integration of machines, people, and information—exemplified by trends such as Industry 4.0, work 4.0, medicine 4.0, education 4.0, service 4.0 (Smart Services) and Artificial Intelligence (AI)—are transforming the business landscape. These megatrends spur innovation but also increase competitive pressures as new market entrants emerge. Within these multiple approaches to combine ICT, humans and products in different dimensions and expressions is the common theme. Through such megatrends, individual innovations as well as innovation projects are initiated by companies of all sizes, research institutes, consulting companies or specialist associations. At the same time, these trends and changes are causing further competitive pressures on SMEs as new players enter their markets. This book attempts to answer as to how German SMEs can maintain their technology leadership, their innovativeness and their competitiveness under these challenging circumstances by using the open innovation approach.

4.3 Driver for Business Success of German Small and Medium-Sized Enterprises

Germany has several drivers of its innovation success. These include its universities as well as research institutes such as the Max Planck Society and the Fraunhofer Institute with which businesses cooperate. In accordance to Smith, Kannabiran and Laing, to Christos Kolympiris and Peter G. Klein as well to Hassan (Hassan, 2024; Kolympiris & Klein, 2017; Smith et al., 2015, pp. 1–3) universities can be an incubator for innovation and entrepreneurship. In total the German university landscape counts 428 educational institutions which employ 36,900 male professors and 15,000 female professors (Statista GmbH, 2025b) (Statista GmbH, 2019)which are divided in universities (109 universities in 2025), universities of applied science (208 in 2025), art schools (52 in 2025), administration universities (30 in 2025), theological universities (16 in 2025) and pedagogical universities (6 in 2025) (Statista GmbH, 2025c). The noteworthy fact is that Germany has more, application-oriented and practice-oriented, universities of applied sciences than other universities. They provide the students with a broad practical knowledge. From the author's experience, the practical training at universities of applied sciences as well as the theoretical education of the student by the universities is mostly supported by regional and local companies, so that the companies deal with relevant topics to practice by the students. In this case, the students are confronted with current issues from the practice-related environment of the companies, which increases the quality of the practical training of the students. The cooperation between the companies and the universities of both types as a critical success factor for German companies.

Another factor is German research institutes. Two of the biggest research institutes are the Max Planck Society and the Fraunhofer Institute. The Max Planck Society operate 84 institutes and facilities to 'conduct basic research in the natural sciences, biology, humanities and social sciences in the service of the general public. The Max Planck Institute is a national and international figurehead for the German research community. More than 6,000 foreign guest researchers and junior researchers work at the various Max Planck Institutes each year' (Max Planck Society, 2025). It conducts 'more than 4,500 cooperation projects of the Max Planck Institutes with more than 5,400 partners in more than 100 countries around the world. With its subsidiary, Max Planck Innovation GmbH, the Max Planck Society ensures that scientific breakthroughs turn into economic successes. The Max Planck Innovation GmbH commercializes patents and technologies and supports founders in the development of new companies based on research findings of the Max Planck Society. Since 1979, the Transfer Agency has overseen about 4,300 inventions and signed more than 2,600 commercialization agreements. Since the beginning of the 1990s, 146 company spin-offs have emerged from the Max Planck Society, of which the overwhelming majority Max Planck Innovation GmbH has actively looked after. The total proceeds for the inventors, the institutes and the Max Planck Society earned around €470 million in the meantime'.

The second major research institute is the Fraunhofer-Gesellschaft. 'Fraunhofer is Europe's largest application-oriented research organization. The research efforts are geared entirely to people's needs: health, security, communication, energy and the environment. As a result, the work undertaken by the researchers and developers has a significant impact on people's lives' (Fraunhofer-Gesellschaft zur Förderung der angewandten Forschung e.V., 2025). Around 70% of the Fraunhofer-Gesellschaft's contract research revenue is derived from contracts with industry and from publicly financed research projects. These strong research units as well as the close cooperation with the companies promote the innovative strength of German companies. Through the cooperation between the companies and the research institutions, know-how, knowledge and new technologies are brought to the companies to create individual products.

A third critical success factor of the German economy is the 'dual vocational training system'. The aim of such an education approach is to build up a theoretical background in combination with a practical training at the same time. The dual training model combines both companies and vocational schools. That means that the trainees will be educated at two places, namely the vocational school and the company. The vocational school will teach theoretical topics which are relevant to the education in the companies. In most cases the trainees are in the vocational school for two days per week, or similar in accordance with the school. The rest of the time is practical training in the companies (Federal Ministry for Economic Affairs and Energy, 2025b). The German dual vocational training system differentiates itself significantly from training systems in other European countries and offers a range of significant advantages for both enterprises and society at large. One of the most prominent benefits is the recruitment of skilled workers, as firms are able to train and retain employees who are already familiar with company-specific processes and values. The unique learning mix of theoretical instruction and practical workplace experience has a demonstrably positive impact on educational outcomes, ensuring that learners acquire both foundational knowledge and applied skills. At the same time, the system strikes a trade-off between broad occupational qualifications and highly job-specific competencies, thereby fostering both flexibility and specialization. Another key aspect lies in the high social acceptance of training, which reflects its established role within the labour market and society. From the perspective of enterprises, vocational training also contributes to cost reduction, as trainees provide productive outputs during their training period. In addition, the system places pressure on schools to adapt their curricula and teaching practices to align more closely with contemporary labour market requirements, thus ensuring relevance and responsiveness. The implementation of broadly accepted minimum quality standards further strengthens the system by safeguarding consistency and reliability across training providers. Finally, one of the most crucial outcomes is the facilitation of a smooth transition from education to employment, which reduces barriers for young people entering the labour market and supports long-term workforce stability.

On the other hand, the dual system of vocational education and training revealed also disadvantages. First, the training market does not always adequately cover the overall training demand, which can lead to mismatches between available training places and the number of applicants. Moreover, the provision of training opportunities is both qualitatively and quantitatively dependent on the willingness and readiness of enterprises to participate in training, thereby creating structural imbalances. A further limitation arises from the fact that the government is required to co-finance education, while at the same time lacking direct control over the design and implementation of training measures. Additionally, the system suffers from insufficient cooperation between teachers in vocational schools and trainers in enterprises, which can hinder the integration of theoretical and practical learning. Maintaining the necessary infrastructure of the dual system also involves considerable formal and administrative effort, adding further complexity. Finally, consistency between educational instruction and company-based training is not always guaranteed, which may undermine the overall coherence and effectiveness of the system.

The fourth success factor is recently established Leading-Edge Cluster. (Bundesministerium für Bildung und Forschung (BMBF), 2022; Federal Ministry of Education and Research, 2015, p. 6), (Federal Ministry of Education and Research, 2015, p. 14). The underlying idea is to foster cooperation between enterprises and research facilities which should lead to improved innovation outcomes (Federal Ministry of Education and Research, 2012; Rubach et al., 2014, p. 17). 'Clusters combine strengths and create synergies which foster research and innovation (Bundesministerium für Bildung und Forschung (BMBF), 2025). With the launch of the Leading-Edge Cluster Competition in 2007, an independent jury selected 15 Leading-Edge Clusters from more than 80 competition entries. These clusters receive funding of up to €40 million over a period of five years. Large corporations, small and medium-sized enterprises, universities and research facilities collaborate on projects such as solutions for energy reforms, digital society or adapting to demographic change' (Federal Ministry of Education and Research, 2015, p. 6) These Leading-Edge Clusters facilitate contacts between companies and research institutes. Through these clusters SMEs and participating companies can also conduct government-funded R&D projects to part-finance innovation projects.

A fifth success factor for the German economy is its specific industries. These include automotive mechanical engineering, chemical, pharmaceutical, food and electrical industries. In terms of investment in innovation in Europe six out of ten companies are from Germany (European Commission, Joint Research Centre, 2019).

Despite these strong drivers on innovation in Germany, German SMEs face multiple challenges to be innovative. The challenges include difficulty in employing well-educated employees especially for digitization. A further obstacle is caused by the flowing out of technological competence and experience due to the buying of German companies by foreign investment companies. One additional innovation issue is the lack of financial resources. Besides this, SMEs also face obstacles in their market penetration. This means that due to more complex technologies,

SMEs need to employ specialists in their sales team to commercialize their products appropriately to the market. For this reason, the question that needs to be answered is how SMEs will maintain their competitiveness and their technology leadership in their individual niches while they face significant environmental challenges.

4.4 The German Economy: Current Status and Future Prospects

According to the European innovation performance scoreboard (EIS) (European Commission, 2024) as shown in Appendix A.1 and in Appendix A.2, Germany occupies an upper-mid position among the **Strong Innovators**, positioned below countries such as Denmark, Sweden, Finland, the Netherlands, and Belgium, but above nations like Cyprus, Estonia, and France which benchmarked against the EU average in 2017, with a direct comparison to the year 2023.

This placement underscores Germany's sustained strength in research, technological development, and industrial innovation, while simultaneously highlighting that its overall performance, though robust, does not reach the very top tier of 'Innovation Leaders' exemplified by the Nordic countries and the Netherlands.

From a European perspective, North-South and West-East divide in innovation performance. Northern and Western European states dominate the upper ranks, with Denmark, Sweden, and Finland demonstrating particularly high levels of innovation capacity, consolidating their long-standing reputations as global leaders in knowledge-intensive industries. In contrast, several Southern and Eastern European member states, such as Romania, Bulgaria, and Greece, fall into the Emerging Innovators category, underscoring persistent structural challenges in research investment, knowledge diffusion, and innovation ecosystems.

Germany's intermediate position within the Strong Innovators cluster indicates that while it remains a central engine of scientific and technological progress in Europe, its performance is increasingly rivalled by smaller yet highly dynamic innovation systems, particularly in Scandinavia and the Benelux region. This suggests that Germany, despite its scale and industrial base, faces the challenge of sustaining agility and adaptability in the rapidly evolving global innovation landscape.

In contrast to 2024 as shown above, Germany ranked on the third place in 2014 and appears within the group of **Innovation Leaders**, alongside countries such as Sweden, Denmark, Finland, and the Netherlands (European Commission, 2014). Its position, while not at the absolute forefront (which is occupied by Sweden, Denmark, and Finland), signals a consistently high level of performance across indicators such as research investment, technological advancement, and the capacity for industrial and organizational innovation.

From a European perspective, the scoreboard shows a clear geographic stratification of innovation capacity. Northern and Western European countries dominate the top ranks, with Sweden standing out as the leading innovator, followed closely by Denmark and Finland. This clustering reflects long-term structural commitments to education, research and development, and strong public-private partnerships in these societies. Germany's placement within this group underscores its central role in maintaining Europe's global competitiveness, particularly as the EU strives to strengthen its position against other major innovation hubs such as the United States and East Asia.

Germany's position relative to other large EU economies, such as France, Italy, and Spain, is particularly noteworthy. France, classified as an Innovation Follower, demonstrates a comparatively weaker performance than Germany. Italy, Slovenia, Czech Republic, Greece, Hungary, Lithuania, Malta, Potugal and Spain, categorized among the **Moderate Innovators**, trail even further behind. This divergence illustrates how Germany maintains a stronger innovation ecosystem within the core group of leading European states, setting it apart from its Southern European counterparts.

The measurement framework of the innovation scoreboard parameter is shown in Appendix A.1. In parallel with the European Innovation Scoreboard (EIS), innovation performance is presented using the European Innovation Performance Index (EIPI). The performance groups of the European Innovation Performance Index are displayed in Appendix A.2. The difference between the European Innovation Scoreboard (EIS) and the European Innovation Performance Index (EIPI) lies primarily in their function and presentation, even though the two are closely linked. The European Innovation Scoreboard is an annual report published by the European Commission that compares the innovation performance of EU member states, other European countries, and selected global competitors. It serves as an analytical tool that measures the state of national innovation systems using 32 indicators in four categories (framework conditions, investment, innovation activities, and impact). The aim is to identify relative strengths, weaknesses, and trends and to support political decision-making. The most important result is the Summary Innovation Index (SII), i.e., the summarized innovation value of a country.

The European Innovation Performance Index (EIPI) is not a standalone measurement system, but rather an aggregate indicator that summarizes and visualizes the results of the scoreboard. It represents the quantitative core of the EIS and shows how well a country performs compared to the EU average. This index is used to form performance groups, i.e., the classification of countries into innovation leaders, strong innovators, moderate innovators, and emerging innovators.

The loss of innovativeness is not the only reason why German companies are not competitive. Industry 4.0, digitization and Artificial Intelligence are current drivers of global innovation and economy growth. However, the German government has been focusing on social policy instead of pursuing sustainable economic policies in recent years. This means the current digitalization supporting infrastructure is poor in Germany in comparison because of the low investment rate in previous years. The World Economic Forum's Networked Readiness Index (NRI) publishes annually the ICT network capability of 133 economies. The NRI analyzes and assesses factors that contribute to development of digital information and communication technologies. Germany is ranked in the ninth place, behind the top countries (1) United States, (2) Singapore, (3) Finland, (4) Sweden, (5) Republic of Korea, (6) The Netherlands, (7) Switzerland and (8) United Kingdom in terms of digital development (Portulans Institute, 2024). Such a low ranking is a bad omen for a strong economy such as Germany because digitization, the associated infrastructure and economic policy constitutes the basis for contemporary economic growth.

A further obstacle for economic growth is visible in the Global Entrepreneurship Monitor (GEM) data. GEM reports the total entrepreneurial activity (TEA) which measures percentage of people in working age population who have either started a business in the last 42 months or who are considering starting a business within the next year (Vyas & Vyas, 2019). According to the Global Entrepreneurship Monitor (GEM) 2024/2025, total early-stage entrepreneurial activity (TEA) in Germany will amount to 9.8% in 2024. This is around a quarter higher than the average of the previous three years and marks a further significant increase in start-up activity in the 18 to 64 age group. For comparison: In 2023, the TEA in Germany was still at 7.7%, the second-highest figure since the GEM surveys began in 1999. With a TEA start-up rate of 9.8% in 2024, Germany is above average in a European comparison, but not at the top. Germany ranks 12th among the 18 EU countries that compare well with Germany and is therefore in the upper midfield. The TEA rate is well above the long-term average in Germany and also significantly above the EU average, but it is surpassed by countries such as Sweden, the Netherlands, Spain and Greece (Hill et al., 2024; Hill et al., 2025).

Another major issue is that many established SMEs are not able to find an appropriate successor. Around 215,000 small and medium-sized enterprises (SMEs) in Germany are actively looking for a succession solution by the end of 2025. This corresponds to around 6% of all SMEs in the country. The average age of the transferor is around 65, which further increases the urgency of the succession issue. In total, around 190,000 to 215,000 companies are due to be handed over in Germany between 2022 and 2026—estimates vary within this range depending on the source and perspective. Only around three quarters of SMEs looking for a successor actually succeed in finding one. In concrete terms, this means that of the 215,000 companies with a short-term need for succession by 2025, around 43,000 companies will probably not be able to arrange their succession and are facing possible closure. This means that around 172,000 SMEs will be able to implement their succession, while more than a fifth will fail. Statistically, one out of seven smaller companies in Germany currently have no succession solution—this corresponds to around 272,000 SMEs in the broader sense, whereby this figure includes longer-term forecasts and small companies. The main reasons for the failure to find a successor are the shortage of suitable successors. This is because 75% of companies state that they have difficulties finding a suitable successor. Age and demographic change are another reason. Over 39% of owners are 60 years or older. The late preparation that many entrepreneurs make when it comes to succession planning exacerbates the active search for a successor (Deutscher Mittelstands-Bund (DMB) e.V., 2025; Fels et al., 2021; Schwartz, 2025).

An additional obstacle for innovation is the low level of investment in education. In the past, social policy was pursued in the political environment rather than pursuing a future-oriented economic and educational policy. For this reason, social security contributions are increasing annually for companies, entrepreneurs and employees. The Investments in education and research by the federal government in 2025 amounts to €22.32 billion in 2025, which corresponds to around 4.7% of the federal budget (Deutscher Bundestag, 2025a; Deutscher Hochschulverband, 2024b). According to government targets, the total share of public and private expenditure on research and development in GDP is 3.5%, Public spending on education, research and science (federal government, federal states, municipalities) amounted to a total of €398 billion in 2023 (Deutscher Hochschulverband, 2024a). The Investment in social benefits and insurance by the federal government in 2025 amounts over 234 billion euros in the 2025 federal budget, which is around 46% of total expenditure (equivalent to over 5% of GDP) (Deutscher Bundestag, 2025b). The largest single item is pension insurance (federal subsidy approx. 122 billion euros), followed by labour market insurance, child benefit, basic income support, citizens' allowance, parental allowance, long-term care, housing benefit and many more. The number of different social insurance in Germany is around 35 benefits, including traditional social insurance benefits as well as numerous individual transfers and subsidies (e.g. child benefit, BAföG, citizen's allowance, basic security, housing benefit, ALG I + II, social assistance, integration assistance, care allowance). Germany in an OECD comparison of investments in education and research according to the OECD, Germany invested around 5.1% of GDP in education (all levels, including private) in 2021, which is slightly below the OECD average of around 5.2%. At around 3.1% of GDP, Germany was well above the European and OECD average for research and development (OECD average: around 2.7% of GDP). The planned increase to 3.5% of GDP in research and development remains one of the leading rates in Europe, but other countries (such as Sweden, South Korea, China) invest even more proportionately (Statistisches Bundesamt, 2025a).

Another hurdle for SMEs is the currently poorly educated graduates. Germany has a distinct landscape of universities, research institutes and an exemplary education system in which companies and schools work together. These are crucial for innovation as well as for economic growth. From the author's experience as the owner of an electronics SME, it can also be said that the education of students in Germany does not meet the requirements of SMEs, because future-oriented topics from the fields of digitization, software development or even mechanical engineering are inadequately taught in the universities. In addition, it is very difficult to train staff due to their lack of general knowledge and numeracy, as well as a lack of proficiency in oral and written German language. This means that the pupils who want to come from the graduating classes into the companies currently do not possess the minimum level of training required by the desired profession. Thus, companies need to provide further in-company training before beginning their apprenticeship. This means that the companies have to teach the new employees the necessary basics in the STEM (Science, Technology, Engineering, and Mathematics) fields by means of suitable internal training measures. In addition, the companies must provide them the practical basic knowledge through further training for their subsequent work. This includes training in use of relevant software development tools, hardware development tools, hardware calculations, circuit calculations and appropriate social behaviour. On top of this newcomers to the profession demand very high salaries. Due to the small number of well-educated and experienced employees, salaries have become too high for a traditional SME to pay. In addition, employees' expectations of benefits in MNC employment such as a company car, retirement plans, supplementary health insurance, flexible working hours, food subsidies or travel allowances are now spilling over to traditional SMEs, which cannot afford to provide them. On the other hand, if SMEs do not offer them, they have greater difficulty in employing well-educated and experienced employees. Almost half of the German companies generally cannot fill vacant jobs with suitably trained specialists (Hardege, 2018, p. 6). At this point, SMEs have three issues to overcome. Well-trained salespeople who have the technical and character ability to sell innovative products and new services (smart services) are very difficult to recruit. Secondly, inability to pay high salaries comparable to those paid by multinational enterprises for such sales specialists. Third, another way to sell new innovations is the internal training of employees. New innovative products or services, especially in the digitalization environment, have to be commercialized through new sales structures instead of using the established sales channels. Furthermore, the distribution process and the stakeholder groups may be different for digital products and for new services than for the distribution of traditional products. It takes a long time to change the established patterns of thinking and behaviour of the sales staff. Many applicants do not fulfil the appropriate mix of technical skills, economic skills and social skills such as written and oral communication, collaboration with others and problem-solving activities (Manpower Group Deutschland, 2018, p. 7).

4.5 Innovation Challenges for Small and Midsized Enterprises

The importance of OI for SMEs is growing steadily. SMEs often focus on search strategies for existing network activities and tend to be more open to known and trusted partners, such as customers and suppliers (Hossain & Kauranen, 2016). The scope of network searches is usually limited by restricted resources. In contrast, universities and intermediary organizations such as living labs or research centres play a central role as innovation supporters. Vertical collaborations (e.g., with suppliers) are particularly relevant for radical innovations, while horizontal collaborations tend to promote incremental innovations. In the field of innovation and technology management, it is evident that SMEs are primarily active in product and technology development (Csath, 2012). A key prerequisite for successful OI is the development of absorptive capacity—that is, the ability to absorb and utilize external knowledge (Spithoven et al., 2011). In addition, intellectual property (IP) protection is of great importance to SMEs, although they are very selective when it comes to patent applications Unlike large companies, SMEs only apply for patents for innovations that have high market potential. A recurring theme is the multitude of challenges that SMEs face in the context of OI. These include limited resources for research and development, unstructured innovation processes, a lack of innovation process expertise, and insufficient access to scientific excellence.

Regardless of the difficulties described, there is a prime example of open innovation in SMEs, which Vanhaverbeke (Vanhaverbeke, 2010) cites, in various examples, how Denmark's SMEs used the open innovation approach to change their business model as well as to create and capture added value. The added value enables the innovative companies to reinvest their profits into the company's growth. The findings of Vanhaverbeke demonstrate that the open innovation approach might also suit traditional SMEs. The open innovation approach contains multiple tools such as 'Crowdsourcing ', 'Innovation Campus', 'Design Thinking', 'Knowledge Management', 'Blue Ocean Method', 'Scenario Technique', 'Cross Industry Innovations' and 'Outcome-Driven Innovation'. These innovation tools, in the context of the open innovation approach, are plausible methods to pursue innovation. Given the great variety of these methods, a traditional SME cannot implement all of them. Furthermore, some methods may not suit the individual needs of German SMEs or the person responsible for innovation may not have adequate knowledge about such innovation tools. Further, intellectual property rights are also a crucial success factor in this context. Nowadays innovations are much more complex. Companies often join together in innovation cooperation to work on individual projects to develop their own products via R&D activities. For this reason, it is important that the right cooperation partnerss are selected well on the one hand and that this cooperative structure is properly managed on the other. Given the SMEs' obvious financial limitations, they have some specific options to finance innovation. Companies should reinvest their profits to finance their innovation projects. Generally investments of profit into innovation follows an appropriate strategy and is dependent on the market position, company size, market segments and corporate goals (Hernández et al., 2015, pp. 71–79). The special features in innovation projects such as a high degree of uncertainty concerning innovation success, and a small proportion of tangible assets might be obstacles to external financing, especially loan financing (Zimmermann, 2014, pp. 3–5). Belitz and Lejpras (Belitz & Lejpras, 2014, pp. 4–6) advise that SMEs finance their innovation from internal funds, mostly by subsidized loans, by means of government-granted subsidized funds, as shown in Fig. 4–5. German government has established several funding opportunities through its subsidized funds. Herewith German SMEs have the ability to partially offset their R&D costs. Such programmes compensate only about 40%–60% (it depends on the innovation programme) of total R&D costs at the company, but they serve as first start-up funding

Table 4.4 Overview of R&D- funding programmes

Funding instrument	Funding body	Target group	Type of funding	Funding amounts
Research allowance	Federal finance	All taxable companies	Tax allowance	25% of labour costs. Max. assessment threshold €12 Mio (from 2026)
ZIM	BMWE	SMEs + Research Institutions	Grant project funding	Up to €3 Mio
SME Innovative	BMFTR	SMEs	R&D projects and pre-commercial R&D project	Guideline of BMBF /BMFTR
IGF / INNO-KOM	BMWE	SMEs + Research Institutions	Grant for preliminary and market research	Up to 90% funding, max. €650.000
Go-Inno	BMWE	SMEs	Consulting and subsidy	50%, max. €50.000

for innovation projects. Over the past few years, the German government has initiated plenty of support measures for companies, enabling them to partially refinance their R&D activities. The following Table 4.4 provides a brief overview of the possible funding projects.

In most cases such innovation funding programmes are available nationwide for SMEs from different sectors (Federal Ministry for Economic Affairs and Energy, 2025c; Federal Ministry of Economics and Technology, 2012, p. 4). Additionally, the Federal Ministry for Economic Affairs and Energy provides a Federal funding database in order to select the appropriate and suitable funding programme (Federal Ministry for Economic Affairs and Energy, 2025a).

Additionally, the demand for intellectual property rights has increased continuously in recent years. This shows that intellectual property rights also play a significant role in innovation, where companies can maintain their individual competitive advantage from innovations. Patent-protected innovation or licensed innovations create added value for the customer and capturing value for the property rights owner company. The common strategy of SMEs is the protection of their knowledge and to make it inaccessible for partners by patents or other property rights. Generally companies have a high interest in having high protection of their intellectual properties (H. Chesbrough, 2024) in the future, because innovation also means a co-development process with external partners, especially for SMEs (Chesbrough et al., 2024). While they cooperate with other companies to process an innovation project the participating companies may use know-how from each other. Intellectual property rights management is very important to avoid tensions in cooperation with other enterprises. The control of property rights and protecting the use of these rights from other firms is very expensive and time-consuming. Therefore, it is necessary to define rules or arrangements from the beginning concerning patenting, co-patents or licence usage. From the author's perspective, intellectual property rights management is crucial for leveraging innovation advantages for German SMEs. An additional option to make new technologies inaccessible for others is the integration of such new technologies into new products that are inaccessible or not visible for potential imitators. For instance, the inaccessibility of new technologies can be performed through new production processes and new production methods such as additive manufacturing processes (Digital Light Processing, MID, 3D printing, etc.) (Macdonald et al., 2014, pp. 234–242; Sloma, 2024; Wolstrup et al., 2025; Yi, Yang, Yue, & Lei, 2025).

To summarize, the protection of intellectual property and the protection of new technologies against imitators is a major challenge for SMEs. On the one hand rules must be created for the use of existing intellectual property during the project period between the partners in cooperative innovation projects. In addition, further rules must be set up as the project consortium circumvents rights arising from this project for the project partners. In addition, companies must protect new technologies from imitators. This is very time-consuming and very expensive because of the involvement of patent attorneys and patent regulations. Furthermore, companies must enforce a granted property right. If another company infringes the property right, the company that owns the property right must legally pursue this infringement and enforce that individual property right. This can be very time-consuming and very expensive for both companies. From the author's perspective, SMEs need to think carefully about whether they want to protect innovation with a traditional right to protect against imitators, or whether newer production processes make it more cost-effective to make innovation inaccessible to other companies.

For successful innovation, networking and collaborating with other companies or research facilities are key. External partners' knowledge and expertise play an important strategic role in the innovation process. Independent experts such as engineering firms, technology consultants, universities or other research institutions can help companies implement innovation projects. Suppliers are also seen as an important external partner for the corresponding innovation projects. In addition, extant research reports that business-to-business partnerships often go far beyond science and technology collaboration and include value creation collaborations which are a new source of knowledge and innovation that the companies could capture (Kumar Singh, 2024; Ritter & Walter, 2024). Overall, the importance of networking and collaboration in the innovation process in general is repeatedly confirmed, especially in respect of SMEs. How such innovation networks are operationally structured depends on by whom and how the network in managed. The network can be structured in the 'hub-spoke' model, which is controlled by a hub company, or in the 'multiplex' model, in which all the companies have more or less an equal voice (Paasi et al., 2010, p. 1048). But in both operational structures an important rule in managing networks is that the central firm must ensure that all partners are better off joining and staying in the network compared to discontinuing the cooperation and leaving the network (Provan et al., 2007; Toigo et al., 2021). That requires activities from the initiating company which supports partners with network information, and they have to support partners who get in trouble during the collaboration. That means that all participants must treat each project partner respectfully and they have to be honest. In addition, the participating project partner has to be strong enough to provide requested input; they must have experience in project organization and project management to succeed in a particular project. Very innovative SMEs show intense engagement in networking which is generally beneficial in foreseeing opportunities and leads to higher innovation. Also needed is to build a trust network between the members. From the author's professional experience, a collaboration between an SME and a large company might be complicated, because SMEs fear that large companies steal technology, they poach employees from the SME, or cheat it. Whereas cooperation on equal sized companies lead to innovation success, because both companies follow the same rules and philosophy in innovating activities. Furthermore, it is important to distinguish between the success measurement of the process implementation itself and the success measurement of the outcome from the innovation activity. One possible approach for the measurement of process-implementation success is the 'Process Enterprise Maturity Model' (PEMM) (Hammer, 2007). The PEMM provides the framework to establish the process structure and guides the development of a process roadmap. However, the outcome of the innovation activity must also be measured to ensure that the invested capital has high returns and I company achieves growth. The evaluation of innovation is influenced from innovation side-effects and the SME must decide what to measure, how to measure and collect the appropriate data. Besides the above-mentionedindividual innovation success measurements, one appropriate performance measurement system might be the 'Net Present Value' (NPV)[2] from a financial perspective. A further performance measurement approach might be the Total Quality Management (TQM) system to measure the SME's performance, their image or their product quality. But such measurement decisions must be made individually by the specific company and cannot be generalized for all companies or for all industries.

4.6 The Concept of Crowdsourcing Platform as an Opportunity for Business Success

As described previously above, innovating SMEs can benefit greatly by cooperating with other companies, universities, research institutes, innovation networks or industry networks. In the process, they can consult appropriate specialists for the relevant innovation projects to get the know-how they need in the company. It is important to involve appropriate people and departments linked with the innovation

[2] The Net Present Value (NPV) is a method for evaluating companies or long-term investment projects. The NPV measures the discounting of future cash returns on an investment to the current moment. The result is a monetary figure

project at an early stage in the innovation activity. It is necessary that the specialist know-how is available to the company and all employees have easy and quick access to the specialists as well as access to the required know-how. For these reasons, this sub-chapter will focus on the crowdsourcing approach as a possible tool for German manufacturing SMEs to usher in open innovation in a targeted and profitable way.

Crowdsourcing means that a heterogeneous, temporally and geographically independent group works together to achieve a common goal. Crowdsourcing is an intrinsic part of the open innovation paradigm. Crowdsourcing is an engaging approach to outsourcing the creation of knowledge and resolving issues to outside participants via a public or semi-public appeal to a broad audience. Typically, creative themes are key, but repetitive tasks can also be performed. Typically, this request is initiated by a website. Crowdsourcing is a community-driven, interactive approach to innovation (Gassmann, 2010, p. 6; Poetz & Sauermann, 2024). This large group can generally be internet users or, more specifically, customers, consumers or members of an online community. The 'optimal' or necessary size of the crowd depends on the type of crowdsourcing project, the nature of the outsourced problem and the information required to solve it (Leimeister & Zogaj, 2013, p. 19). Crowdsourcing tries to use the principle of wisdom of crowds and its benefits. Behind this principle, there is the idea that in certain circumstances a group of people can achieve better results than individuals. The term 'the crowd' here represents an undefined mass of people or problem solvers. Such mass of people or problem solvers come mostly from outside the company to solve a defined issue. Two types of crowdsourcing can be distinguished: tournament collaboration versus collaborative crowdsourcing. In the first case, the members of the crowd choose their own tasks and work independently. In the second case, members of the crowd seek other members with whom they collaborate to solve the problems (Afuah & Tucci, 2012, p. 355).

The process begins with the crowdsourcer, which can be an individual, an organization, or an industrial enterprise. The crowdsourcer initiates the process by outsourcing tasks or projects that require external input, knowledge, or labour (Leimeister, Durward, & Zogaj, 2016, p. 16; Poetz & Sauermann, 2024). These tasks are then transferred to the intermediary or agent, which is represented by the crowdsourcing platform. The platform functions as the central hub, facilitating the interaction between the crowdsourcer and the contributors. It provides the digital infrastructure necessary for the dissemination of tasks, the collection of solutions, and the overall management of the process. Finally, the tasks reach the crowdworkers, a diverse group of individuals who execute the assignments. Crowdworkers provide their skills, knowledge, and labour, often distributed across different geographical locations. Their collective contributions represent the essential output of the crowdsourcing process. There are more than 536 platforms available (Statista GmbH, 2013), globally reflecting a high number of job opportunities that are becoming increasingly important for employees and crowdworkers.

The crowdsourcing platforms can be divided into four categories. The classification of crowdsourcing platforms can be distinguished according to their primary areas of application and the types of activities they facilitate. Research and development platforms are designed to address questions and challenges related to innovation processes, providing solutions to complex research problems. Marketing and design platforms focus on creative tasks such as the development of websites, logos, or comprehensive marketing campaigns, thereby supporting companies in enhancing their market presence. Freelancer platforms serve as intermediaries between companies and independent professionals, enabling the outsourcing of diverse tasks such as reviewing websites, verifying web links, or drafting press releases. While these activities are often practical and necessary, they are typically less innovative in nature. Finally, idea creation platforms specialize in generating solutions across a wide range of industries, tackling heterogeneous problems and offering innovative input for business development.

Additionally, there are many intermediary platforms accessible which provide different applications as shown in Table 4.5 till Table 4.9. The following tables display the different intermediary platforms, which represent a sample of accessible crowdsourcing platforms and innovation platforms worldwide.

It is obvious that most crowdsourcing and innovation platforms are operated from the United States of America or Canada. A smaller number of such platforms are operated from Germany or the European Union. Crucially, most platforms are available in the English language.

The growing incorporation of artificial intelligence into these platforms presents significant opportunities on one side. AI algorithms currently execute standard tasks, help assess submitted concepts, and manage the workflow between clients and crowdworkers. Crowdsourcing is crucial, especially in data labelling, which serves as the foundation for technical AI systems. Platforms like Shaip and Clickworker concentrate primarily on data processing via human involvement to enhance AI-driven systems (Healthly.AI Data, L., 2022). Innovative platform methods similarly employ learning systems to evaluate the quality of human inputs, choose participants according to their abilities, or allocate tasks intelligently. Nonetheless, employing AI on crowdsourcing platforms presents various risks for providers, users, and the crowd as a whole. A major issue is the absence of transparency in AI systems concerning contributors. Numerous choices—like task allocation or assessment—are determined by opaque algorithms whose standards remain undisclosed. This may result in unjust treatment, incorrect conclusions, or bias, particularly if the AI relies on biased or inaccurate training data (Glöckner, 2024). The protection of data and the security of information are also vital concerns. Crowdworkers frequently manage sensitive information, such as in healthcare, without adequate guidance or defined legal criteria. The circumstances become especially sensitive when AI systems create links between participant profiles, performance trends, and private data.

Conclusion: Platforms for crowdsourcing, when integrated with artificial intelligence, are significant contributors to the digital economy and research. They facilitate large-scale data processing and gathering, foster innovation and engagement, and greatly enhance AI progress. Concurrently, though, risks like transparency issues, unequal distribution, data security, and ethical norms require improved

Table 4.5 Research-and Development platforms intermediary platforms, based on (Gassmann, 2010)

Type of intermediary platform	Name of intermediary platform	Web address	Application	Country	Language
Research-and Development platforms	InnoCentive	www.innocentive.com	Problem solving scientific-based questions	USA	English
	TekScout	N.A.	Problem solving scientific-based questions	N.A.	N.A.
	IdeaConnection	www.ideaconnection.com	Idea creation platform	Canada	English
	Yet2.com	www.yet2.com	Trade platform for copyrights	USA, UK, Japan	English, Japanese
	PRESANS	www.presans.com	Problem solving scientific-based questions	France	English
	Hypios	www.hypios-ci.com	Problem solving scientific-based questions	France	French
	NineSigma	www.ninesigma.com	Platform for solving technical issues	Japan, Belgium, USA	English
	Pharma Licensing	www.pharma Licensing.com	Platform for Technology Scouting, Technology Marketing and Government & Education which is related to the pharmaceutical industry.	USA, UK	English

regulation. In the absence of clear guidelines, there is potential for exploitation, algorithmic bias, and a decline in trust in these emerging types of work.

SMEs might be ready to use appropriate crowdsourcing platforms to solve to specific innovation issues if suitable crowdsourcing platforms are available. The main reason for the lack of use of crowdsourcing platforms by the traditional German manufacturing SME is their lack of understanding of the opportunities and potential benefits from the use of such platforms. This in turn is caused by a combination of issues, including the language in which the platforms are provided, their geographical locations and lack of evidence of good management of a German crowdsourcing project. In addition, some platforms communicate their

Table 4.6 Marketing and Design Platforms intermediary platforms, based on (Gassmann, 2010)

Type of intermediary platform	Name of intermediary platform	Web address	Application	Country	Language
Marketing and Design Platforms	RedesignMe	http://www.redesignme.com	Logo design and corporate design	The Netherlands, USA	English
	Idea Bounty	https://www.ideaconnection.com/outsourcing/idea-bounty-23.html	Marketing competitions, marketing activities	N. A	English
	crowdSPRING	http://www.crowdspring.com	Logo design and corporate design	USA	English
	Battle of concepts	https://www.battleofconcepts.nl	Innovation concepts can be challenged by the crowd.	The Netherlands	Dutch / English
	Brand Tags	NA.	Platform to share knowledge and experiences about markets	N.A.	N.A.
	Guerra Creativa	https://www.guerra-creativa.com/en/	Crowdsourcing platform for logos, websites and more	Argentina	Spanish, Portuguese, English
	99designs	https://www.99designs.de/	Platform for Logo-Design, Website-Design, Print-Design, T-Shirt Print-Design	Germany	German

(continued)

Table 4.6 (continued)

Type of intermediary platform	Name of intermediary platform	Web address	Application	Country	Language
	12designer	Was taken over by 99designs	Platform for Logo-Design, Flyer-Design, Website-Design	Germany	German
	Logo Arena	https://www.logoarena.de/	Platform for a company-logo competition by 50 or more suggestion which created the individual company logo	Canada	German, English

services and their approach in such a way that for the SMEs the focus of services is not always obvious or understandable at the first glance. From the marketing point of view, SMEs that have never dealt with crowdsourcing before will not be picked up on these platforms. Further, most of the traditional German SMEs are family-managed and are run either an old or a young person. Due to the education in the younger generation, for them the language in which the crowdsourcing platform is provided is no barrier to post an idea or an issue which can be solved on such a platform. However, the elderline generation company owners are not likely to use it due to the language barriers, or mentality-based constraints.

It should also be borne in mind that IP protection must be inbuilt on such platforms and the SMEs should receive solutions targeted to their problems or access to an appropriate innovation network which could provide specialized ideas closely related to the SMEs' issue.

The alternatives to the crowdsourcing platforms might be innovation networks, industry networks, the chamber of commerce, business consultancies, or specific internet forums. However, none of these are as effective and efficient as crowdsourcing platforms for the SMEs and other stakeholders to manage their innovation projects.

As with any new technological provision, the crowdsourcing phenomenon contains advantages but also risks that companies should be aware of. A further advantage is the revival of internally rejected ideas and incorporation of customer needs and market impulses in the development of new products. Crowdsourcing has also associated risks. The overall costs of a crowdsourcing project including its hidden costs are much higher than those of crowdsourcing itself. It is, therefore, important not to use crowdsourcing projects as a single action but as part of an overall strategy, and to provide the necessary financial and human resources. Another issue is crowdworker motivation, because the low level of compensation

Table 4.7 Platforms for freelancer intermediary platforms, based on (Gassmann, 2010)

Type of intermediary platform	Name of intermediary platform	Web address	Application	Country	Language
Platforms for freelancer	Amazon Mechanical Turk	www.mturk.com	Simple activities	USA	English
	Spudaroo	https://www.crunchbase.com/organisation/spudaroo-com	Virtual advertising copywriter	Canada	English
	HumanGrid	Belongs to CLICKWORKER	Minor online-activities	N.A	N.A.
	TopCoder	https://www.topcoder.com/	Crowdsourcing platform for Design &P prototyping of technical products, Software-Application development, Development of Algorithms & Analytics	USA	English
	LeadVine	https://www.leadvine.com/	'LeadVine' is an online social community that simplifies how companies find new customers. Search listings and make money with the information that you already have".	N.A.	N.A.
	AppJobber	https://www.appjobber.de/	AppJobber is a crowdsourcing platform for fast and cost-effective data collection in retail and other business-relevant locations.	Germany	German, English, Spanish, French, Italian, Polish, Portuguese, Turkish
	Clickworker	https://www.clickworker.de/	Small online tasks such as web research, surveys, keywording etc.	Germany	German, English
	cash4feedback	N.A	N.A.	N.A.	N.A.
	Freelancer.com	http://www.freelancer.com	'Outsource anything you can think of!'	Australia	English,

Table 4.8 Idea creation platforms intermediary platforms, based on (Gassmann, 2010)

Type of intermediary platform	Name of intermediary platform	Web address	Application	Country	Language
Idea creation platforms	Atiso	www.atiso.com	Crowdsourcing with its own innovation community	Switzerland	German
	Big Idea Group	http://www.thinkbigideagroup.com/	Innovators for ideas, marketing and products	USA	English
	Exnovate	https://www.exnovate.org/	Open innovation in a network	Belgium	English
	Chaordix	www.chaordix.com	Chaordix is a global leader in collaborative innovation and they are working with brands. As early adopters of crowdsourcing technology, the proven ability to build collaborative communities, combined with the proprietary software and methodology.	Canada	English
	Innovation Exchange	http://www.ixa.nl/en/home.html	Platform for collaborative research, Science Incubator, Licensing and collaboration opportunities	The Netherlands	English

(continued)

Table 4.8 (continued)

Type of intermediary platform	Name of intermediary platform	Web address	Application	Country	Language
	Idea Crossing	http://www.innovationsmethoden.info/experten/idea-crossing-inc	Idea Crossing specializes in organizing ideas competitions and innovation contests for its customers with the help of the "Challenge Accelerator" software tool	USA	English
	Jovoto	www.jovoto.com	Mass collaboration on the Jovoto platform leads to fresh ideas, from product design and marketing campaigns to innovative business scenarios of the future.	Germany	English
	crowdINNO	N.A.	Platform on which competitions for innovations can be advertised	N.A.	N.A.
	Innovationskraftwerk	www.innovationskraftwerk.de	Open Innovation Platform, which not only deals with innovation and problem-solving processes in business but also scientific and socio-political issues.	Germany	German, English

and the fact that the participants generally have to relinquish all rights to their solutions can sometimes limit their personal interest in an optimal solution. A further risk might be the legal framework. The participants of a crowdsourcing project want to benefit from the market success of their idea, but the companies usually try to get the sole rights to the ideas. It is essential to communicate this clearly in advance and provide the crowdworker with an appropriate, reliable and transparent legal framework in regard to the IP management.

Table 4.9 German-based crowdsourcing platforms; based on (Leimeister et al., 2016)

Category	Name of intermediary platform	Web address	Application	Location	Language
Micro-task platform	1. Clickworker 2. Mylittlejob	1. www.clickworker.com 2. www.mylittlejob.com	1. Small online tasks such as web research, surveys, keywording etc. 2. Small tasks such as transcriptions, text writing, translations	Germany	German
Marketplace platform	1. Crowd Guru 2. Content.de	1. www.crowdguru.de 2. www.Content.de	1. Small tasks such as content for online-shops, website construction, text writing 2. Text writing for SEOs, blogger, online-shops, translations	Germany	German
Design platform	1. 12designer 2. designenlassen.de	1. Was taken over by 99designs 2. www.designenlassen.de	Platform for Logo-Design, Flyer-Design, Website-Design 2. Logo design, Web-design, Flyer-design	Germany	German
Testing platform	1. Applause 2. Testbirds	1. www.applause.com 2. www. testbirds.com	1. Crowd Testing, Automated testing, payment testing, accessibility testing 2. Testing of websites, testing of wearables, testing of mobile apps, testing of games	Germany	German
Innovation platforms	1. Jovoto 2. UnserAller	1. www.jovoto.com 2. www.crowdcommunity.de	Mass collaboration on the Jovoto platform leads to fresh ideas, from product design and marketing campaigns to innovative business scenarios of the future.	Germany	German

4.7 Critical Examination of the Open Innovation Approach

Open innovation is not a new paradigm; it has been discussed in innovation management literature since the 1960s. A company's innovation progress depends heavily on the quality of external information (Trott & Hartmann, 2009, pp. 715–716). At the same time, there is a central risk inherent in the open innovation approach: the outsourcing of R&D activities. This could lead to companies losing critical core competencies to external partners (Trott & Hartmann, 2009, p. 720).

When SMEs collaborate with large corporations, they must ensure that they retain their intellectual property and make it inaccessible to others for maintaining and enhancing their own market share. Otherwise, the SMEs face the risk that the large companies will take undue advantage and they may lose the developed technology and the associated property rights. However, such collaborations are a chance for SMEs to generate additional income through a smart licence system. The open innovation concept is not perfect, as it may involve a potential leakage of knowledge outflow. On the one hand, companies can collaborate with one another to maintain their market share and sustain their competitive advantage and on the other hand, collaborating companies can ensure that they keep their own intellectual property. This applies also to the developed technologies, for which appropriate property rights can be registered if necessary. This implies an openness of the strategic alignment by the company in case of intellectual property management. Intellectual property rights management is crucial for innovation advantage, especially for German SMEs. Furthermore, the integration of new technologies into new products in such a way that they are inaccessible or invisible to potential imitators, because protecting intellectual property from other firms enables the companies to get access to new markets and enhance their technological position, build up their reputation, gain market share, attract third-party contribution and grow the market. Finally, it can be summarized that a certain degree of openness is required for the success of a collaboration. In particular, when companies are involved in an innovation network, it is crucial how open the company is, because in innovation networks, all partners rely on the openness of the network members to carry out corresponding R&D projects. It is equally important that SMEs in particular retain their know-how and do not lose it through collaborations with large companies. The companies involved, therefore, must decide their particular degree of openness depending on the situation and make it dependent on the trust they have built in others. Appropriate contracts must also be signed prior to cooperation which regulate the use of IP as well as the use of knowledge and technologies during the R&D project period and beyond.

4.8 Summary of the Chapter

The German companies invest significant amount of their turnover in innovation activities in many industries, which provides them competitive advantage vis-à-vis their domestic and international competitors. In addition to this, the German economy comprises of an extended local manufacturing value chain which is vital in creating business growth and prosperity for both the German companies and the population. Along with this economic structure, the German economy is helped by two large research facilities, the Max Planck Society and the Fraunhofer Institute. In addition, the German economy has a diverse landscape of universities and universities of applied sciences which collaborate closely with the research facilities and the companies. The German economy is also aided by the German 'dual vocational training system' in which pupils receive both practical training on the job and advanced theoretical training in schools. A further relevant driver of the business innovativeness is the establishment of Leading-Edge Clusters by the German government across the country. Such Leading-Edge Clusters act as competence centres for innovation collaborations and innovation hubs for both multinational enterprises and SMEs.

Notwithstanding these positive aspects, the German economy faced major setbacks in its innovativeness in European comparisons and it declined to be ranked as a 'Strong Innovator' instead of an 'Innovation Leader' that it used to be in the previous years. The German economy also lost ground in its competitiveness in the worldwide comparison. In addition, the German economy and the German companies lost ground in the 'Network Readiness Index', which measures and assesses the factors, policies and institutions that enable a country to fully leverage information and communication technologies (ICTs) for increased competitiveness and well-being. One other difficulty for the German economy is that many company owners do not find an appropriate successor to run their business in the future. As a result, the companies are either closed or sold to foreign investors. A further obstacle to German companies' innovativeness and competitiveness is poorly educated employees, which is caused by less investments in education and research activities while major investments will be found in social insurance by the Federal Government. This led the schools and universities to be underfunded, churning out inadequately educated graduates. The companies consequently had to cope with the lack of skilled workers and still try to maintain their market share and competitiveness. Under these circumstances, open innovation may be a useful opportunity for German SMEs.

Open innovation approach contains multiple innovation tools such as 'Crowdsourcing', 'Innovation Campus', 'Design Thinking', 'Knowledge Management', 'Blue Ocean Method', 'Scenario Technique', 'Cross Industry Innovations' and 'Outcome-Driven Innovation' The tool 'crowdsourcing' is offered by intermediaries who bring the crowdworker and the crowdsourcer together through an online platform. The intermediaries act as 'brokers' to connect the knowledge seekers (crowdsourcer) and the knowledge provider (crowdworker) by providing the necessary infrastructure for the crowdsourcing activities. The crowdsourcing platforms can be divided into different categories based on their objectives such as for marketing purposes, for idea creation purposes or for R&D purposes. For this reason, this tool might be appropriate for SMEs and the following chapters explore and explain how the open innovation approach and therewith one particular innovation tool—the crowdsourcing concept—can be designed to support the SMEs' innovation activities.

References

Afuah, A., & Tucci, C. L. (2012). Crowdsourcing As a Solution to Distant Search. *Academy of Management Review, 37*(3), 355–375. https://doi.org/10.5465/amr.2010.0146

Belitz, H., & Lejpras, A. (Eds.) (2014). Financing Patterns of Innovative SMEs and the Perception of Innovation Barriers in Germany [Special issue]. *German Institute for Economic Research,* 2014.

Bundesministerium für Bildung und Forschung (BMBF) (2022). *Bundesbericht Forschung und Innovation 2022 - Hauptband.*

Bundesministerium für Bildung und Forschung (BMBF) (2025). Technologisch souverän in Deutschland und Europa.

Chesbrough, H. (2024). Open Innovation: Accomplishments and Prospects for the Next 20 Years. *California Management Review, 2024*(67), 164–180. https://doi.org/10.1177/00081256241273964

Chesbrough, H., Radziwon, A., Vanhaverbeke, W., & West, J. (2024). The Oxford Handbook of Open Innovation (1st ed.). Oxford University Press.

Csath, M. (2012). Encouraging innovation in small and medium sized businesses: learning matters. *Development and Learning in Organizations: An International Journal, 26*(5), 9–13. https://doi.org/10.1108/14777281211258635

Deutsche Bundesbank (2025). The Bundesbank's forecast for Germany: Economic recovery slowly getting started. Retrieved from https://www.bundesbank.de/en/press/press-releases/the-bundesbank-s-forecast-for-germany-economic-recovery-slowly-getting-started-959308

Deutscher Bundestag (2025a). Haushalt 2025: Etat für Bildung und Forschung steigt leicht. Retrieved from https://www.bundestag.de/presse/hib/kurzmeldungen-1015438

Deutscher Bundestag (2025b). Haushaltsentwurf 2025 zugeleitet. Retrieved from https://www.bundestag.de/presse/hib/kurzmeldungen-1097400

Deutscher Hochschulverband (2024a). Ampelkoalition grundsätzlich einig über Haushalt. Retrieved from https://www.forschung-und-lehre.de/politik/ampelkoalition-grundsaetzlich-einig-ueber-haushalt-6518

Deutscher Hochschulverband (2024b). Einsparungen beim BMBF ab 2026. Retrieved from https://www.forschung-und-lehre.de/politik/einsparungen-beim-bmbf-ab-2026-6537

Deutscher Mittelstands-Bund (DMB) e.V. (2025). Lagebericht bei der Unternehmensnachfolge. Retrieved from https://www.mittelstandsbund.de/kompetenzbereiche/nachfolge/beitrag/lagebericht-bei-der-unternehmensnachfolge

European Commission (2014). Innovation Union Scoreboard 2014.

European Commission (2024). *European Innovation Scoreboard 2024.*

European Commission, Joint Research Centre (2019). The 2018 EU Industrial R&D Investment Scoreboard. Retrieved from https://ec.europa.eu/growth/industry/innovation/facts-figures/scoreboards_en

Federal Ministry for Economic Affairs and Energy (2025a). Ihr Weg zum passenden Förderprogramm. Retrieved from https://www.foerderdatenbank.de/FDB/DE/Home/home.html

Federal Ministry for Economic Affairs and Energy (2025b). Training in Germany. Retrieved from https://www.make-it-in-germany.com/en/study-vocational-training/training-in-germany

Federal Ministry for Economic Affairs and Energy (2025c). Vorwettbewerbliche Forschung für den Mittelstand: IGF und INNO-KOM - Industrieforschung für Unternehmen. Retrieved from https://www.bundeswirtschaftsministerium.de/Redaktion/DE/Artikel/Technologie/vorwettbewerbliche-forschung-fuer-den-mittelstand.html

Federal Ministry of Economics and Technology (2012). *Central Innovation Programme for SMEs: Boosting innovation.* Central Innovation Programme for SMEs—Funding for innovation.

Federal Ministry of Education and Research (2012). Regional vernetzt, global erfolgreich: Spitzencluster für mehr Innovation und Wettbewerbsfähigkeit. *Bundesministerium für Bildung und Forschung (BMBF).*

Federal Ministry of Education and Research (2015). Deutschlands Spitzencluster Germany's Leading-Edge Clusters. *Bundesministerium Für Bildung Und Forschung (BMBF),* 1–49.

Federal Ministry of Justice and Consumer Protection (2015). Handelsgesetzbuch, Stand 31.8.2015 I 1474.

Fels, M., Suprinovič, O., Schlömer-Laufen, N., & Kay, R. (2021). *Unternehmensnachfolgen in Deutschland 2022 bis 2026: Daten und Fakten Nr.27* (1st ed.). *Daten und Fakten.* Institut für Mittelstandsforschung Bonn.

Fraunhofer-Gesellschaft zur Förderung der angewandten Forschung e.V. (2025). The Fraunhofer-Gesellschaft. Retrieved from https://www.fraunhofer.de/en/about-fraunhofer/profile-structure.html

Glöckner, L. (2024). Die problematische Lieferkette von Anwendungen Künstlicher Intelligenz. Retrieved from https://www.recyclist-magazin.de/post/lieferkette-von-kuenstlicher-intelligenz

Hammer, M. (2007). The Process Audit. *Harvard Business Review, April* 2007, 111–123.

Hardege, S. (2018). Fachkräfte gesucht wie nie!_DIHK-Arbeitsmarktreport 2018. *DIHK-Arbeitsmarktreport 2018, 2018,* 1–30. Retrieved from https://www.dihk.de/isuche?SearchableText=DIHK Arbeitsmarktreport 2018.

Hassan, N. A. (2024). University business incubators as a tool for accelerating entrepreneurship: theoretical perspective. *Review of Economics and Political Science., 9,* 434–453. https://doi.org/10.1108/REPS-10-2019-0142

Healthly.AI Data, L. (2022). Crowd Workers for Data Collection—an Indispensable Part of Ethical AI. Retrieved from http://shaip.com/blog/crowd-workers-for-data-collection-an-indispensable-part-of-responsible-ai/

Hernández, H., Hervás, F., Tübke, A., Vezzani, A., Dosso, M., Amoroso, S., … Gkotsis, P. (2015). The 2015 EU Industrial R&D Investment Scoreboard. EUR—Scientific and Technical Research series –, 2015. doi:https://doi.org/10.2791/50785.

Hill, S., Friedl, C., Guerrero, M., Ionescu-Somers, A., Coduras, A., Menipaz, E., … Shay, J. (2025). *GEM 2024/2025 Global Report: Entrepreneurship Reality Check.*

Hill, S., Ionescu-Somers, A., Coduras, A., Guerrero, M., Menipaz, E., Boutaleb, F., … Shay, J. (2024). *GEM 2023/2024 Global Report: 25 Years and Growing.*

Hossain, M., & Kauranen, I. (2016). Open innovation in SMEs: a systematic literature review. *Journal of Strategy and Management, 9*(1), 58–73. https://doi.org/10.1108/JSMA-08-2014-0072

IfM Bonn (2025). Mittelstand im Überblick: Kennzahlen der KMU nach Definition der EU-Kommission. Retrieved from https://www.ifm-bonn.org/statistiken/mittelstand-im-ueberblick/kennzahlen-der-kmu-nach-definition-des-ifm-bonn/kennzahlen-deutschland

Institut für Mittelstandsforschung Bonn. (2000). Gründungen und Unternehmensschließungen. Retrieved from https://www.ifm-bonn.org/statistiken/gruendungen-und-unternehmensschliessungen/unternehmensinsolvenzen#:~:text=im%201.%20Halbjahr%202025%20auf%20rund%2012.000%20gestiegen

Kolympiris, C., & Klein, P. G. (2017). The Effects of Academic Incubators on University Innovation. *Strategic Entrepreneurship, 2017*(11), 145–170. https://doi.org/10.1002/sej.1242

Kumar Singh, A. (2024). Creating Value in a Business Ecosystem. *Journal of Creating Value, 10*(1), 8–10. https://doi.org/10.1177/23949643241256412

Leimeister, J. M., Durward, D., & Zogaj, S. (2016). *Crowd worker in Deutschland: Eine empirische Studie zum Arbeitsumfeld auf externen Crowdsourcing-Plattformen. Study / Hans-Böckler-Stiftung: Nr. 323.* Düsseldorf: Hans-Böckler-Stiftung.

Leimeister, J. M., & Zogaj, S. (2013). Neue Arbeitsorganisation durch Crowdsourcing: Eine Literaturstudie. *Econstor, 2013.* Retrieved from http://hdl.handle.net/10419/116744

Macdonald, E., Salas, R., Espalin, D., Perez, M., Aguilera, E., Muse, D., & Wicker, R. B. (2014). 3d Printing for the Rapid Prototyping of Structural Electronics. *IEEE Access, 2*, 234–242. https://doi.org/10.1109/ACCESS.2014.2311810

Manpower Group Deutschland (2018). Lösungen für den Fachkräftemangel, *2018.* Retrieved from https://www.manpowergroup.de/neuigkeiten/studien-und-research/studie-fachkraeftemangel/

Max Planck Society (2025). A portrait of the Max Planck Society. Retrieved from https://www.mpg.de/short-portrait

Paasi, J., Valkokari, K., Luoma, T., Hytönen, H., Nystén-Haarala, S., & Huhtilainen, L. (2010). Innovation Management Challenges of a System Integrator in Innovation Networks. *International Journal of Innovation Management*l, *14*(06), 1047–1064. https://doi.org/10.1142/S1363919610003008

Poetz, M. K., & Sauermann, H. (2024). *How and When to Involve Crowds in Scientific Research.* Edward Elgar Publishing.

Portulans Institute (Ed.) (2024). *Network Readiness Index 2024.* Retrieved from https://networkreadinessindex.org/

Provan, K. G., Fish, A., & Sydow, J. (2007). Interorganizational Networks at the Network Level: A Review of the Empirical Literature on Whole Networks. *Journal of Management, 33*(3), 479–516. https://doi.org/10.1177/0149206307302554

Ritter, T., & Walter, A. (2024). Value Creation in Business-to-Business Relationships. *Elgar Encyclopedias in Business and Management Series, 2024*, 314–316. https://doi.org/10.4337/9781035307319.ch58

Rubach, S., Johansen, F. R., & Andersson, G. (2014). Missing Actions in Cluster Innovation. *International Journal of Advanced Corporate Learning (iJAC), 7*(1), 17. https://doi.org/10.3991/ijac.v7i1.3524

Schwartz, M. (2025). Nachfolge-Monitoring Mittelstand 2024: Jedes vierte Unternehmen denkt über Geschäftsaufgabe nach. *KfW Research Fokus Volkswirtschaft, 2025*, 1–9. Retrieved from https://www.kfw.de/PDF/Download-Center/Konzernthemen/Research/PDF-Dokumente-Fokus-Volkswirtschaft/Fokus-2025/Fokus-Nr.-481-Januar-2025-Nachfolge.pdf

Simon, H. (2007). Hidden Champions des 21. *Die Erfolgsstrategien unbekannter Weltmarktführer*. Campus Verlag.

Sloma, M. (2024). Additive Manufacturing of Structural Electronics. *De Gruyter*. https://doi.org/10.1515/9783110793604

Smith, S., Kannabiran, G., & Laing, S. (2015). Strategic Positioning of IT Business Incubators within Universities - A Comparative Study of the United Kingdom and India. *38th ISBE Conference 2015, 2015.*

Spithoven, A., Clarysse, B., & Knockaert, M. (2011). Building absorptive capacity to organise inbound open innovation in traditional industries. *Technovation, 31*(1), 10–21. https://doi.org/10.1016/j.technovation.2010.10.003

Statista GmbH (2013). Anzahl der aktiven Crowdfunding-Plattformen* weltweit von 2010 bis 2012. Retrieved from https://de.statista.com/statistik/daten/studie/258185/umfrage/anzahl-der-crowdfunding-plattformen-weltweit/

Statista GmbH (2019). Anzahl der hauptberuflichen Professoren und Professorinnen an deutschen Hochschulen 1999 bis 2017. Retrieved from https://de.statista.com/statistik/daten/studie/160365/umfrage/professoren-und-professorinnen-an-deutschen-hochschulen/

Statista GmbH (2025a). Annual average unemployment rate in Germany from 2005 to 2025. Retrieved from https://www.statista.com/statistics/227005/unemployment-rate-in-germany/

Statista GmbH (2025b). Anzahl der hauptberuflichen Professoren und Professorinnen an deutschen Hochschulen von 2000 bis 2023. Retrieved from https://de.statista.com/statistik/daten/studie/160365/umfrage/professoren-und-professorinnen-an-deutschen-hochschulen/

Statista GmbH (2025c). Anzahl der Hochschulen in Deutschland in den Wintersemestern 2018/2019 bis 2024/2025 nach Hochschulart. Retrieved from https://de.statista.com/statistik/daten/studie/247238/umfrage/hochschulen-in-deutschland-nach-hochschulart/

Statista GmbH (2025d). Höhe der Innovationsausgaben der Unternehmen in Deutschland in ausgewählten Branchen im Jahr 2023. Retrieved from https://de.statista.com/statistik/daten/studie/7588/umfrage/innovationsaufwendungen-nach-branchen-in-deutschland/

Statista GmbH (2025e). Höhe der Innovationsausgaben der Unternehmen in Deutschland in ausgewählten Branchen im Jahr 2023. Retrieved from https://de.statista.com/statistik/daten/studie/7588/umfrage/innovationsaufwendungen-nach-branchen-in-deutschland/

Statista GmbH (2025f). Monthly unemployment rate in Germany from May 2024 to May 2025. Retrieved from https://www.statista.com/statistics/1304278/unemployment-rate-monthly-germany/

Statistisches Bundesamt (2025a). Basistabelle öffentliche Gesamtausgaben für Bildung. Retrieved from https://www.destatis.de/DE/Themen/Laender-Regionen/Internationales/Thema/Tabellen/Basistabelle_BildAusg.html

Statistisches Bundesamt (2025b). Gross domestic product: detailed economic performance results for the 1st quarter of 2025. Retrieved from https://www.destatis.de/EN/Press/2025/05/PE25_182_811.html

Statistisches Bundesamt (2025c). Mehr Unternehmensinsolvenzen im 1. Halbjahr 2025 als im 1. Halbjahr 2024. Retrieved from https://www.destatis.de/DE/Presse/Pressemitteilungen/2025/09/PD25_332_52411.html#:~:text=12%20009%20beantragte%20Unternehmensinsolvenzen.

Statistisches Bundesamt (2025d). National accounts, domestic product. Retrieved from https://www.destatis.de/EN/Themes/Economy/National-Accounts-Domestic-Product/_node.html

Toigo, T., Wegner, D., Da Silva, S. B., Zarpelon, F., & d. M. (2021). Capabilities and skills to orchestrate innovation networks. *Innovation & Management Review, 18*(2), 129–144. https://doi.org/10.1108/INMR-10-2019-0126

Trott, P., & Hartmann, D. (2009). Why Open Innovation is old wine in new bottles. *International Journal of Innovation Management, 13*(4), 715–736.

Vanhaverbeke, W. (2010). The Benefits of Open Innovation in Low-Tech SMEs: The Quilts of Denmark Story. *Innovation Management, 2010*(1).

Verband der Vereine Creditreform e. V. (2025). Insolvenzen in Deutschland, 1. Halbjahr 2025. Retrieved from https://www.creditreform.de/aktuelles-wissen/pressemeldungen-fachbeitraege/news-details/show/insolvenzen-in-deutschland-1-halbjahr-2025#:~:text=im%201.%20Halbjahr%202025%20auf%20den%20h%C3%B6chsten%20Stand%20seit%20zehn%20Jahren

Vergabeblog.de (2024). Über 99% aller Unternehmen der Privatwirtschaft sind KMU. Retrieved from https://vergabeblog.de/2024-08-15/ifm-bonn-ueber-99-aller-unternehmen-der-privatwirtschaft-sind-kmu/

Vyas, V., & Vyas, R. (2019). Entrepreneurship and economic growth: A review and synthesis of conceptual arguments and empirical evidence. *International Review of Entrepreneurship.*

Wollmershäuser, P. D. T. (2025). ifo Economic Forecast Spring 2025: German Economy Treading Water. Retrieved from https://www.ifo.de/en/facts/2025-03-17/ifo-economic-forecast-spring-2025-german-economy-treading-water

Wolstrup, A. F., Spangenberg, J., Yamamoto, A., Gleadall, A., & Zsurzsan, G. (2025). Advances in 3D printed electromechanical sensors: Performance comparison, trends, and future directions. Additive Manufacturing, 106, 104799. doi:https://doi.org/10.1016/j.addma.2025.104799.

Zimmermann, V. D. (2014). Kfw SME Panel 2013: How German SMEs finance their innovations. *KFW ECONOMIC RESEARCH, 50*(3), 1–7.

How Small and Medium-Sized Enterprises Can Become More Innovative and What Measures Need to Be Taken to Achieve

5

5.1 Introduction and the Rationale for Innovation Activities

This chapter summarizes the research findings of the semi-structured in-depth interviews and provides an overview of the measures required to enable companies to pursue innovative approaches and deal with the research summary. Firstly, the sub-chapter deals with the research findings of the semi-structured in-depth interviews and shows the statistical evaluation of the online survey. These results are statistically evaluated using a one-sample t-test, their positive or negative values as well as for their statistical significance. These one-sample t-tests are carried out for all considered industries, as well as for all company sizes.

As already described above, crowdsourcing has been identified as an appropriate tool for open innovation for German SMEs in this thesis. For this, the book displays some related crowdsourcing platforms through a 'Target Product Profile Analysis' and based on the findings of this analysis conceptualized a new crowdsourcing platform for German SMEs. This new platform's conceptualization has been informed by the results of the 'Target Product Profile analysis'.

5.2 Driving Competitiveness and Resilience: The Strategic Role of Innovation in Small and Medium-Sized Enterprises

Innovation activities are a crucial growth factor for small and medium-sized enterprises (SMEs). By developing new products, improving processes, or adopting novel business models, SMEs can differentiate themselves from competitors, access new markets, and increase efficiency. Innovation also enhances adaptability, enabling firms to respond effectively to technological and economic changes. Thus, continuous innovation not only drives competitiveness and productivity but

M. Vathauer, *Breaking Barriers with Open Innovation in Germany*, Management for Professionals, https://doi.org/10.1007/978-3-032-14660-1_5

also secures long-term growth and resilience in an increasingly dynamic and knowledge-based economy. The following sub-chapters deal with these aspects in detail and dig deeper into innovation activities.

5.2.1 Innovation as a Strategic Imperative: Securing Competitiveness in the Face of Global and National Pressures

Small and medium-sized enterprises (SMEs) are under increasing competitive pressure from multinational corporations and foreign companies within their industry sectors. These foreign competitors often benefit from country-specific cost advantages, allowing them to offer similar products at lower prices. National competitors, particularly larger firms, may also enjoy structural advantages such as greater market penetration, superior human and financial resources, and organizational scale. Consequently, SMEs must rely heavily on innovation to secure their long-term market position and survival. Innovation, therefore, emerges as a strategic imperative for these firms.

All surveyed SMEs acknowledged the strategic relevance of innovation, with most indicating that it is concretely embedded in their corporate strategies. The firms go as far as to integrate innovation 'very concretely' into their strategic frameworks. The rationale for such emphasis varies: international competition is a key motivator, prompting some companies to actively involve various stakeholders in the innovation process. The minority number of firms highlighted the inclusion of younger employees to capture generational perspectives.

Despite variations in implementation, all SMEs surveyed affirmed that innovation constitutes a core business objective. However, only a subset explicitly defined innovation as part of their corporate mission. The integration of both short- and long-term innovation strategies is considered essential to adapting to dynamic market conditions and evolving customer needs. It is therefore recommended that innovation management and strategy be fully aligned with broader corporate goals.

Operationally, the initiation of innovation projects often begins within the sales and development teams, ensuring responsiveness to market changes. Nonetheless, ultimate decision-making authority rests with senior management. Several firms stressed the importance of leveraging technological knowledge and experience gained from previous projects to inform new developments. This iterative approach allows companies to offer customized product solutions and sustain innovation-driven growth. Finally, all firms concurred that innovation is either an 'important' or 'very important' driver of business growth, particularly as a response to price competition and rising customer expectations regarding product and process innovation.

5.2.2 Innovation as a Strategic Necessity: How Small and Medium-Sized Enterprises Balance Customer Expectations, Competitive Pressures, and Sustainable Growth

Small and medium-sized enterprises (SMEs) often operate in highly competitive market environments that demand continuous innovation to ensure survival and sustain customer satisfaction. For most of the surveyed firms, innovation is not optional but a strategic necessity driven by both external pressures—such as pricing and technological competition—and internal objectives related to efficiency and customer expectations.

Across the board, SMEs emphasized that innovation is essential to meet evolving customer demands and to optimize production processes, particularly to maintain competitive pricing. While some firms are motivated by direct customer expectations for innovation, others innovate to remain technologically and economically viable in response to aggressive competition. For instance, process innovation is often pursued to improve cost efficiency, particularly in industries like automotive manufacturing, whereas in other sectors, customer expectations may demand a high degree of product customization and innovation.

The majority of the surveyed SMEs actively pursue innovation with the goal of developing proprietary products or services. This pursuit is critical for enhancing market penetration and reducing dependency on client-driven service models. SMEs with their own product portfolios can access new market segments and achieve greater independence. Firms frequently involve customers, end-users, or external development partners in the innovation process to tailor solutions closely to market needs.

The concept of innovation is multifaceted and varies by company. It may encompass the creation of entirely new products, services, or processes, as well as the enhancement of existing ones. Business model innovation and diversification, while acknowledged, play a less central role for most firms. The dominant forms of innovation among the SMEs are product and process innovation. These activities have demonstrably improved competitiveness and helped firms maintain their market positions.

The minority number of interviewed companies adopt a dual approach by simultaneously creating new offerings and improving existing technologies or workflows. This allows them to remain agile and responsive to shifting market dynamics. In some cases, the development of new products and services has led to the emergence of new business models, although this is less commonly a core focus.

The motivation for innovation among SMEs is diverse and strategically complex. It includes aims such as quality and technology leadership, market consolidation, and competitiveness preservation. The minority number of surveyed SMEs consider market or cost leadership as realistically attainable, particularly given the structural limitations typical of smaller firms. Instead, innovation is often seen as a mechanism to sustain or slightly advance their competitive position. While one firm did express a clear ambition towards market leadership, most recognized that traditional SMEs may not have the capacity to reach such positions and thus focus on attainable goals such as revenue growth, product quality, and process efficiency.

In summary, innovation serves SMEs not only as a strategic tool for maintaining relevance and customer satisfaction but also as a pathway to moderate growth, specialization, and resilience in increasingly volatile markets.

5.2.3 Cultivating Innovation Culture in Small and Medium-Sized Enterprises: Balancing Resource Constraints, Employee Engagement, and Strategic Investment

Innovation culture plays a pivotal role in enabling and sustaining innovation activities within small and medium-sized enterprises (SMEs). It encompasses multiple dimensions, including management's encouragement of employee-driven innovation, the allocation of responsibility for innovation, employee integration into innovation initiatives, and the internal communication of innovation successes. In the surveyed SMEs, innovation is most commonly driven by the managing director, often in conjunction with the head of research and development. None of the surveyed firms, however, had appointed a dedicated innovation manager or established an innovation department, largely due to resource constraints typical of traditional German SMEs.

Innovation within SMEs is influenced by either a technological or commercial orientation. The former prioritizes technical solutions, whereas the latter emphasizes rapid return on investment. Internal innovation processes typically involve multiple stakeholders, including the sales force, development, marketing, and senior management. However, only one individual usually holds ultimate responsibility for the innovation outcome.

The majority of firms reported involving key personnel such as the managing director, product managers, development heads, and line managers. Employees from production and sales are also frequently engaged due to their direct contact with customers and insights into practical implementation. In contrast, marketing departments are generally underrepresented in innovation processes. Only a minority of firms involved the finance or controlling departments, which may be due to the absence of formal controlling functions in many SMEs. In such cases, financial oversight responsibilities are often assumed by other roles, such as accounting or the managing director.

Employee involvement across departments is viewed as essential for successful innovation. Firms that engage employees from the early stages of a project tend to achieve better outcomes. This inclusion also extends to departments not traditionally associated with innovation, such as production or purchasing, as these employees can offer critical insights into feasibility and implementation. Involvement practices vary: some firms include employees based on topic relevance, while others engage them systematically from the project's inception.

Communication of innovation success within the company is another key element of innovation culture. Recognizing employee contributions fosters motivation and supports the generation of new ideas. While some companies provide incentives and internal recognition for innovation, others rely solely on informal encouragement. The minority number of firms reported structured support or reward systems, with the remainder offering little to no formalized backing. Nevertheless, internal recognition through meetings or project updates is common and helps reinforce the value of employee contributions.

Despite limited structured funding, most SMEs provide their employees with time and space to explore innovative ideas during regular working hours. Investment in human resources for innovation varies, with some firms allocating up to 49% of their workforce to innovation-related tasks. Time for creativity is recognized as important, though often not formally integrated into working hour models or individual performance objectives. Some firms offer fixed percentages of work time for innovation and creativity, while others provide ad hoc flexibility depending on the project.

Financial investment in innovation among the surveyed SMEs ranges from 1% to 15% of annual turnover, with most reinvesting around 10%. This financial commitment reflects the strategic significance of innovation within these organizations and indicates a tangible resource allocation despite limited budgets.

Finally, in collaborative innovation efforts, SMEs often maintain oversight of external innovation partners. Most firms monitor partner contributions throughout the project to ensure alignment with goals and minimize risk. This control mechanism is particularly emphasized as projects progress, with some SMEs applying structured oversight from the outset to safeguard project success.

In summary, innovation culture in SMEs is shaped by limited resources, cross-functional employee engagement, informal yet meaningful recognition, flexible time allocation for idea development, and cautious financial and partnership management. Despite these constraints, SMEs demonstrate a pragmatic and adaptive approach to fostering innovation within their organizational frameworks.

5.2.4 Navigating Informal Processes, External Pressures, and Intellectual Property Challenges

In contrast to multinational corporations, which typically implement well-structured and formalized innovation processes embedded within broader innovation ecosystems, traditional small and medium-sized enterprises (SMEs) generally lack such formal frameworks. Among the SMEs surveyed, the minority reported having a defined innovation process for developing new products, while the remaining enterprises operated without a formal structure. Instead, innovation activities are often initiated in response to customer requests or are guided by internal standard parameters, resulting in an unstructured or ad hoc approach to innovation.

Although most SMEs do not have internally defined innovation processes, several follow structured procedures when participating in government-subsidized projects. In such cases, compliance with externally prescribed funding guidelines effectively substitutes for an internal innovation framework. Only a minority of SMEs have integrated partial innovation processes within their Quality Management Systems in line with DIN EN ISO 9001:2015. Despite this, employees in most of these firms are not fully aware of these processes.

The role of intellectual property rights (IPR) is another critical component of the innovation process, albeit one that is unevenly emphasized across SMEs. For most respondents, IPR—including copyrights, patents, trademarks, and brand names—is considered important for protecting innovations, supporting marketing strategies, and establishing a competitive advantage. Nevertheless, SMEs often face substantial challenges in enforcing these rights, particularly in international contexts. Limited resources restrict their ability to monitor markets or pursue legal action against infringement. Some SMEs attempt to accelerate market entry for new products as a strategy to counter rapid imitation, especially from international competitors.

While SMEs own patents and use trademarks to differentiate themselves, the minority number of firms has embedded the treatment of intellectual property rights within its innovation process in a structured way. In most cases, the handling of copyrights is inconsistent or reactive, often determined by the specific demands of a customer project rather than by internal policy.

In summary, the innovation processes in traditional SMEs are largely informal and project-specific, shaped more by external demands and funding opportunities than by internal strategic planning. Employees are seldom fully integrated into defined innovation workflows, and intellectual property protection, while recognized as important, is typically handled in an ad hoc manner. This fragmented approach limits the potential for systematic innovation management and underscores the structural constraints that many SMEs face in building a robust, repeatable innovation infrastructure.

5.2.5 From Innovation to Market: Commercialization Pathways, Barriers, and Strategic Challenges

The commercialization of newly developed products or services plays a crucial role in the innovation strategy of small and medium-sized enterprises (SMEs). For the majority of SMEs surveyed, commercialization occurs immediately upon the completion of the innovation project.

Timing of commercialization varies across SMEs and may occur at different stages of the innovation process—prior to completion, immediately afterwards, or years later. The minority number of SMEs commercialize products even before finalizing the innovation process to allow integration of customer-specific requirements. Others aim for rapid commercialization upon project completion to meet cost-efficiency goals. In certain cases, commercialization is dependent on customer demand or the readiness of the associated production processes, which may extend the timeline by six months to a year.

Market entry barriers remain a significant challenge for SMEs attempting to bring innovations to market. These include entrenched competitors, pricing pressure, regulatory hurdles, and difficulties obtaining necessary certifications. Some firms also suffer from incorrect market assessments or face resistance from customers unwilling to adopt new technologies. These barriers limit the ability of SMEs to capitalize fully on their innovations despite technical or conceptual advancements.

The financial contribution of innovations to overall company turnover varies widely. For the majority of interviewed SMEs, products developed within the past five years contribute significantly—ranging from 11% to over 30%—to annual revenues. However, this contribution is often inconsistent and influenced by factors such as customer readiness, product complexity, and internal management expectations. Generally the firms reported they are unable to quantify the precise turnover share attributable to recent innovations, reflecting either a lack of internal tracking or the long-tail nature of commercialization outcomes.

In summary, while SMEs tend to commercialize innovations rapidly and often in direct collaboration with customers, they face structural limitations in licensing, market access, and quantifying the financial impact of innovation. These constraints highlight the importance of aligning innovation management with commercial strategy, customer engagement, and regulatory planning to ensure long-term return on innovation investments.

5.2.6 The Measurement of Innovation Success

Key Performance Indicators (KPIs) are widely acknowledged as effective tools for evaluating the outcomes of innovation processes within small and medium-sized enterprises (SMEs). Several SMEs identified 'innovation turnover'—the share of revenue derived from innovative products—and its contribution to overall profitability as key metrics for assessing innovation success. Additionally, some firms consider the number of intellectual property rights, such as copyrights, and the degree to which innovations impact existing products and processes as meaningful indicators.

Although there are numerous established methods to measure both the innovation process and its implementation, practical application among SMEs remains inconsistent. The measurement of innovation success is very fragmented. The minority of interviewed firms using a multi-faceted approach, including innovation turnover, the number of copyrights obtained, and the effect of innovations on established product and process frameworks, while an other small number of companies had predefined KPIs, including the extent to which innovations influenced existing operations and their transferability to future projects or new product developments. In contrast, some companies rely solely on innovation turnover as a success metric, while others do not measure innovation outcomes at all.

Despite these individual efforts, none of the surveyed SMEs regularly apply structured KPIs in a consistent manner. This lack of systematic measurement indicates a gap between recognizing the value of performance indicators and fully integrating them into the innovation management process. As a result, the potential benefits of data-driven innovation evaluation—such as strategic alignment, performance improvement, and informed decision-making—remain underutilized in many SMEs.

5.2.7 Navigating Open Innovation in SMEs: Challenges and Opportunities for Structured Implementation

The open innovation approach, frequently employed by multinational enterprises, is generally recognized among small and medium-sized enterprises (SMEs), although practical understanding and application remain limited. The minority number of interviewed SMEs had encountered the term 'open innovation' through sources such as advanced technology cluster events, conferences hosted by institutions like Fraunhofer, or through online platforms. However, only a few respondents were able to provide a coherent explanation of the concept. One SME had not heard of the term at all.

While open innovation encompasses a variety of structured tools—such as crowdsourcing, design thinking, scenario techniques, and outcome-driven innovation—awareness and usage of these instruments among SMEs are low. The most commonly recognized tools were 'scenario technique' and 'knowledge management', followed by limited familiarity with 'crowdsourcing'. Methods such as 'design thinking', 'blue ocean strategy', and 'cross-industry innovation' were rarely known, and 'outcome-driven innovation' was entirely unfamiliar to all surveyed SMEs. None of the respondents reported consistent use of innovation tools within their organizations. Some had considered using such tools, but implementation was hindered by a lack of knowledge or the dominance of daily operational demands.

With respect to sources of input for innovation, the SMEs indicated reliance on internal experience. In addition, most draw input from customers, employees, and collaborations with universities. Participation in innovation networks and engagement with competitors, research institutions, or suppliers serve as supplementary sources for some firms, although these are less frequently utilized.

The use of third-party intellectual property, such as licenses or copyrights, which is a common component of open innovation strategies, is limited among the surveyed SMEs. A minority number firms reported actively using such licences—primarily for software development or product customization—due to cost-effectiveness. The remaining SMEs either do not engage with third-party intellectual property at all or use it only for standardized, non-innovative applications.

In conclusion, while the concept of open innovation is nominally familiar to many SMEs, substantial knowledge gaps persist, and practical application of its tools is minimal. Innovation processes within these firms remain largely internal, experience-driven, and are seldom supported by structured innovation methodologies or external intellectual property assets.

5.2.8 Pragmatic Partnerships: How to Navigate Regional Collaboration Within the Open Innovation Paradigm

Collaboration with external partners is a fundamental aspect of the open innovation paradigm, wherein small and medium-sized enterprises (SMEs) expand their organizational boundaries to integrate external knowledge and expertise. The majority of the surveyed SMEs engage in cooperation with customers and suppliers. A minority of SMEs maintain partnerships with universities or research facilities. External development service providers are involved in some cases, while none of the SMEs cooperate with competitors, start-ups, or spin-offs—cooperation types more common among multinational corporations.

To formalize and secure these collaborative arrangements, SMEs often implement specific contractual measures. Several firms rely on individual cooperation agreements combined with non-disclosure agreements (NDAs) to safeguard intellectual property and define roles within joint projects. However, the application of such legal instruments varies: some firms negotiate only NDAs, others apply both NDAs and cooperation contracts, and one firm engages in collaborations without formal agreements.

Geographically, SMEs predominantly cooperate on a regional or national level. All surveyed companies reported regional and national partnerships. Cooperation efforts are most frequently directed towards regional universities and innovation partners, especially in southern Germany.

Regarding the acquisition of innovation partners, most SMEs rely on innovation networks, which play a central role in initiating partnerships. High-performance networks such as cutting-edge technology clusters, as well as recommendations from other firms, serve as the main channels for partner identification. The majority number of interviewed SMEs also establish partnerships through connections with local universities or through participation in public tenders, although the latter remains relatively rare.

In summary, SMEs tend to pursue a pragmatic and regionally focused approach to external collaboration, shaped by accessibility, trust, and practical constraints. While formal mechanisms for cooperation exist, their usage is inconsistent, and the full strategic potential of broader open innovation ecosystems remains underutilized in the SME context.

5.2.9 Innovation Financing: Government Grants Between Opportunity and Bureaucratic Burden

Small and medium-sized enterprises (SMEs) have access to various financing options (see Appendix A.3.) for innovation activities, including crowdfunding, reinvestment of profits, bank loans, and government grants. Notably, all surveyed SMEs had previously utilized government grants to support their innovation projects. However, despite their widespread use, these grants are widely perceived as unattractive due to the considerable administrative burden involved. This administrative complexity has been identified by most SMEs as the primary obstacle in accessing such funding. Moreover, based on the author's professional experience, government grant programmes vary in terms of funding quotas and never cover 100% of the innovation costs incurred by SMEs.

In practice, SMEs encounter multiple challenges in navigating government-funded programmes. While some are experienced in identifying and applying for relevant grants, they often rely on support from innovation networks to locate suitable funding opportunities. Even for those familiar with the procedures, the high administrative workload significantly limits the attractiveness and feasibility of these programmes. SMEs generally pursue government grants only when such activities do not interfere with the progress of ongoing innovation projects.

The majority number of SMEs reported that the disproportionate administrative demands result in an unfavourable cost–benefit ratio. Although these programmes can provide partial financial relief, their procedural complexity and inefficiency frequently lead to dissatisfaction and deter SMEs from frequent or future participation. Consequently, while government grants remain a formally available innovation financing mechanism, their practical utility for SMEs is constrained by systemic bureaucratic barriers.

5.3 Navigating Innovation in Small and Medium-Sized Enterprises: Leveraging Agility and Culture for Competitive Advantage

The Table 5.1 summarizes which aspects are important to the surveyed SMEs with regard to their innovation activities and why SMEs undertake innovation activities. The SMEs do not implement a structured innovation process they implement innovation projects as shown above. As a result, SMEs often do not realize that they have significant competitive advantage due to their ability to react quickly and target market changes and customer requirements.

However, few of them run innovation projects to become a market leader, a cost leader or a technology leader. Furthermore, the SMEs do not run business model innovation. If they run an innovation project, they involve multiple stakeholders within the company such as the employees from the production, sales and R&D department, the line manager and the manager at the early stages of the project. Additionally, the interviewed SMEs try to build up an innovation culture in which

Table 5.1 Summarizing of the results of the semi-structured in-depth interviews

No	Item	Result
1	Importance and nature of 'innovation'	**'Innovation' is very important** for SMEs and is a core **objective** of their strategy. Furthermore, innovation is a **driver for company growth**. The SMEs do not follow a **structured innovation process**
2	Reason for innovation	SMEs execute innovation projects to **develop new products or new services** or to **improve existing products incrementally**. Furthermore, they also execute **process innovation** to **maintain their market share** **Cost leadership, technology leadership and quality leadership** are the goals of innovation projects. **Market leadership is NOT**
3	Innovation culture	The SMEs involve internal stakeholders such as **employees from the R&D department, from the sales department and the line managers** as well as external stakeholders **from the beginning** of the innovation process SMEs **support and communicate individual innovation success** internally and provide **room for innovation** to their employees
4	Commercialization of innovations	SMEs **commercialize their innovations early**. Intellectual **property rights are important to them**. They face problems in ensuring property rights. The SMEs **do not licence their innovations to others** for commercial use
5	Measurement of innovation success	SMEs **measure their innovation success** by appropriate KPIs
6	Open innovation and tools	SMEs **have some knowledge** of open innovation and of the related tools. SMEs receive **new ideas** for their innovation activities **from their own experiences,** as well as through their interactions with **universities, research facilities and customers** SMEs mainly **cooperate with their local customers** SMEs find external innovation partners mainly through **innovation networks or cutting-edge technology clusters**
7	Financing of innovation	SMEs mainly use **government subsidies and their own profits** to execute innovation projects. Alternative financing tools are used less often

the employees are given room for their innovation, in which the employer grants financial resources for employee innovation and communicates innovation success within the company to motivate them for innovation. Furthermore, some of the SMEs have knowledge about the open innovation approach to some extent, but they do not properly know the tools for such an approach such as crowdsourcing, blue ocean method, scenario technique, cross-industry innovation, or outcome-driven innovation. The SMEs run innovation projects to maintain competitiveness, maintain market share and generate business growth.

5.4 Quantitative Insights into Innovation Dynamics of German Small and Medium-Sized Enterprises

This sub-chapter presents the findings of analysis of information generated by the questionnaire used to conduct a quantitative survey of German SMEs. The aim of the survey was to determine if the findings that emerged from the qualitative interviews are generalizable to the larger population of manufacturing SME in Germany. To be able to conduct such a survey, 45,609 SMEs across Germany have been surveyed in eight different industry sectors. The industries have been selected by the European Industrial R&D Investment Scoreboard (European Commission, 2016). Depending on the nature of questions the data coding scheme shown in Table 5.2 'Data coding scheme for evaluating the quantitative questionnaire' below has been used. By giving negative values to unfavourable responses, it became easy to identify—just by looking at the mean values of the response data—if there was agreement or disagreement with the prepositions inherent in a specific survey question.

Figure 5.1 Shows the distribution by industry segments of the surveyed SMEs.

The survey data reveals a disproportionate representation across various industry sectors as shown in Fig. 5.1 'Industry segments of the surveyed small and medium-sized enterprises'. The majority of respondents originate from the software and computer services sector, accounting for 34.8% of the total sample. This is followed by the manufacturing sector, which is also notably represented with 20.2%. In contrast, the pharmaceutical industry is significantly underrepresented, comprising only 1.9% of respondents. Other sectors with moderate representation include mechanical engineering (16.0%), automotive and automotive supply

Table 5.2 Data coding scheme for evaluating the quantitative questionnaire

Data coding				
−2	−1	0	1	2
Strongly disagree	Disagree	Neutral	Agree	Strongly agree
Never	Seldom	Sometimes	Often	Always
Very unsuitable	Unsuitable	Cannot say	Suitable	Very suitable

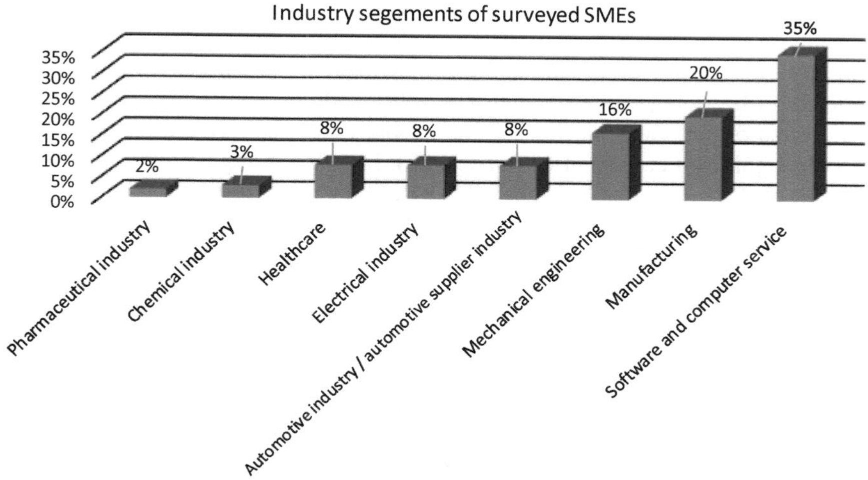

Fig. 5.1 Industry segments of the surveyed small and medium-sized enterprises

(8.4%), electrical industry (8.0%), healthcare (7.6%), and the chemical industry (2.9%).

In terms of company size measured by number of employees, the data shows a strong dominance of smaller SMEs: 84.1% of all surveyed enterprises have 1–50 employees. A further 7.3% fall into the 51–100 employee range, 2.2% have 101–150 employees, and 1.6% employ between 151 and 200 people. Only 4.6% of surveyed SMEs employ between 201 and 249 individuals. This distribution underscores the prevalence of micro and small enterprises within the surveyed sample across all industry sectors.

5.4.1 Contribution of New Product Development to Revenues

The analysis reveals that nearly all surveyed companies engage in new product development (NPD), with varying degrees of revenue contribution. The distribution of revenue derived from NPD is relatively balanced: 20% of businesses report a revenue contribution of 1–10%, while another 20% indicate that more than 50% of their revenue is attributable to NPD. Other companies fall within intermediate ranges, with 15% reporting 11–15% revenue contribution, 17% reporting 16–20% revenue contribution, 16% reporting 21–30% revenue contribution, and 12% indicating 31–40% of revenue generated through new product development.

Descriptive statistics on innovation-related activities and strategic intentions show generally positive engagement with innovation. Most companies report actively pursuing product innovation (mean = 1.04) and process innovation (mean = 0.54), while business model innovation is significantly less common, indicated by a negative mean (−0.23). Strategic intentions lean heavily towards quality leadership (mean = 0.96), technology leadership (mean = 0.60), market leadership (mean = 0.22), and maintaining competitiveness (mean = 1.57), while cost leadership (mean = 0.07) is notably less prioritized.

In terms of perceived barriers to innovation, customer expectations emerge as the only significant constraint (mean = 0.23). In contrast, regulation (−0.27), certification (−0.19), protection rights (−0.84), and import restrictions (−1.16) are generally not seen as obstacles. These findings are confirmed by the results of a one-sample t-test, which highlights statistical significance across nearly all variables except for cost leadership intention, which was found to be statistically insignificant ($p = 0.225$). The test results further reinforce that companies are focused on product and process innovation, driven by objectives such as quality, market, and technology leadership, while largely dismissing external regulatory and legal barriers as major impediments to innovation.

5.4.2 Bridging Strategic Commitment and Cultural Gaps: Employee Involvement and Organizational Support for Innovation in German Manufacturing Small and Medium-Sized Companies

The analyses of innovation culture in German manufacturing SMEs reveal key insights into employee involvement and organizational support for innovation. A one-sample t-test indicates that innovation culture is characterized by selective inclusion of leadership and varying degrees of support for employee-driven innovation initiatives.

The results show statistically significant and positive engagement of R&D heads (mean difference = 0.29, $p < 0.001$) and production heads (mean difference = 1.08, $p < 0.001$) in innovation activities. Moreover, companies actively provide time (mean = 0.86, $p < 0.001$) and financial resources (mean = 0.43, $p < 0.001$) to employees for innovation-related tasks. Importantly, innovation successes are communicated to employees, as reflected in a strong positive mean (1.21, $p < 0.001$), indicating that companies value transparency and recognition of innovative outcomes.

However, the findings also highlight significant deficiencies. There is a strong negative tendency against promoting employee-initiated innovation (mean = −1.08, $p < 0.001$), and companies do not provide dedicated working spaces for innovation (mean = −1.09, $p < 0.001$). These results suggest a lack of structural and motivational support for bottom-up innovation processes.

In terms of managerial involvement, the engagement of marketing heads is statistically significant but moderate (mean = 0.22, $p = 0.01$), while the involvement of sales heads is statistically insignificant and slightly negative (mean = −0.04, $p = 0.600$). This implies that innovation tends to be driven more from technical and operational functions rather than customer-facing departments.

Overall, while German manufacturing SMEs show a degree of strategic commitment to innovation by involving key technical leaders and allocating resources, there are notable cultural and structural barriers that limit broader employee engagement in the innovation process.

5.4.3 Selective Engagement and Untapped Potential: Open Innovation Practices in German Manufacturing Small and Medium-Sized Enterprises

The analysis of open innovation practices in German manufacturing SMEs, based on the one-sample t-test and reveals a fragmented and selective engagement with contemporary innovation concepts and external collaboration strategies.

The results in Table 5.3 shown, the respondents are generally familiar with the terms *open innovation* (mean = 0.84, $p < 0.001$), *crowdsourcing* (mean = 0.14, $p = 0.06$), and *knowledge management* (mean = 0.53, $p < 0.001$). However, there is limited awareness of other strategic innovation concepts. Specifically, there is a lack of familiarity with *design thinking* (mean = −0.20, $p = 0.01$), *innovation campus* (mean = −0.50, $p < 0.001$), *market-driven methods* (mean = −0.14, $p = 0.07$), and especially the *blue ocean method* (mean = −1.19, $p < 0.001$), indicating a significant gap in exposure to certain innovation frameworks.

In terms of actual usage, the situation is more pronounced. Respondents show a strong reluctance or absence of practice when it comes to employing open innovation methods such as *crowdsourcing* (mean = −1.46, $p < 0.001$), *innovation campus* (mean = −1.59, $p < 0.001$), *design thinking* (mean = −0.68, $p < 0.001$), *knowledge management* (mean = −0.35, $p < 0.001$), *blue ocean method* (mean = −1.52, $p < 0.001$), and *market-driven methods* (mean = −0.62, $p < 0.001$). This reflects a generally low adoption rate of structured innovation methodologies within the sector.

With respect to partnership development, the data show that innovation partners are primarily found through *innovation networks* (mean = 0.41, $p < 0.001$), *technology clusters* (mean = 0.63, $p < 0.001$), and *calls for tender* (mean = 0.84, $p < 0.001$). Additionally, collaboration with *competitors* (mean = 0.63, $p < 0.001$), *investors* (mean = 0.50, $p < 0.001$), *the state* (mean = 0.66, $p < 0.001$), and *development service providers* (mean = 0.23, $p < 0.001$) plays a notable role in the innovation ecosystem. There is also a marginally significant relationship with *companies from other industries* (mean = 0.11, $p = 0.08$).

In contrast as shown in Table 5.3, partnerships based on *recommendations* (mean = −0.22, $p < 0.001$), on *customer projects* (mean = −0.24, $p < 0.001$) or on *clients-cooperation* (mean = −0.70, $p < 0.001$), on *suppliers-cooperation* (mean = −0.18, $p = 0.01$), on *university-cooperation* (mean = −0.04, $p = 0.52$), on *research institutions-cooperaiton* (mean = 0.03, $p = 0.62$), and *employees innovation* (mean = −0.64, $p < 0.001$) are less relevant or statistically insignificant. This suggests that external innovation collaborations are selective and often do not

Table 5.3 One-Sample t-Test on general open innovation

One-Sample t-Test						
	Test Value = 0					
	t	df	Sig. (2-tailed)	Mean Difference	95% Confidence Interval of the Difference	
					Lower	Upper
Heard the term open innovation	12.84	370	0.000	0.840	0.71	0.96
Heard of crowdsourcing	1.86	370	0.060	0.140	−0.01	0.28
Heard of innovation campus	−7.18	370	0.000	−0.500	−0.63	−0.36
Heard of design thinking	−2.66	370	0.010	−0.200	−0.35	−0.05
Heard of knowledge management	7.75	370	0.000	0.530	0.4	0.67
Heard of blue ocean method	−19.49	370	0.000	−1.190	−1.31	−1.07
Heard of market-driven method	−1.83	370	0.070	−0.140	−0.29	0.01
Used crowdsourcing	−29.01	370	0.000	−1.460	−1.56	−1.36
Used innovation campus	−36.78	370	0.000	−1.590	−1.68	−1.51
Used design thinking	−8.95	370	0.000	−0.680	−0.83	−0.53
Used knowledge management	−4.59	370	0.000	−0.350	−0.5	−0.2
Used blue ocean method	−29.97	370	0.000	−1.520	−1.61	−1.42
Used market-driven method	−7.81	370	0.000	−0.620	−0.77	−0.46
Contribution to innovation work with others	−9.55	369	0.000	−0.630	−0.76	−0.5
Found partner through innovation networks	5.42	369	0.000	0.410	0.26	0.56
Found partner through technology cluster	8.65	369	0.000	0.630	0.49	0.78
Found partner through calls for tender	11.14	369	0.000	0.840	0.69	0.99
Found partner through recommendations	−3.37	369	0.000	−0.220	−0.35	−0.09

(continued)

Table 5.3 (continued)

One-Sample t-Test						
	Test Value = 0					
	t	df	Sig. (2-tailed)	Mean Difference	95% Confidence Interval of the Difference	
					Lower	Upper
Found partner through customer projects	−3.52	369	0.000	−0.240	−0.37	−0.1
Clients as innovation partner	−10.13	369	0.000	−0.700	−0.84	−0.56
Suppliers as innovation partner	−2.70	369	0.010	−0.180	−0.31	−0.05
Competitors as innovation partner	9.21	369	0.000	0.630	0.5	0.77
Research facilities as innovation partner	0.50	369	0.620	0.030	−0.09	0.16
Universities as innovation partner	−0.65	369	0.520	−0.040	−0.17	0.09
Investors as innovation partner	6.66	369	0.000	0.500	0.35	0.64
The state as innovation partner	9.82	369	0.000	0.660	0.53	0.79
Companies from other industries as innovation partner	1.78	369	0.080	0.110	−0.01	0.22
Development services provider as innovation partner	3.38	369	0.000	0.230	0.09	0.36
Employees as innovation partner	−9.74	369	0.000	−0.640	−0.77	−0.51
Market study before innovation	−3.62	369	0.000	−0.200	−0.3	−0.09
Influencing innovation partner to achieve innovation goals	−4.66	369	0.000	−0.240	−0.35	−0.14

include the broader stakeholder network typically associated with open innovation models.

Moreover, SMEs show limited strategic integration of innovation, as evidenced by the absence of *market studies prior to innovation* (mean = −0.20, $p < 0.001$) and the lack of *active influence on partners to achieve innovation goals* (mean = −0.24, $p < 0.001$).

In conclusion, German manufacturing SMEs demonstrate a cautious and selective approach to open innovation. While some external partnerships are leveraged, particularly with structured networks, clusters, and institutional actors like the state or investors, there is minimal application of modern innovation tools and limited engagement with broader stakeholder collaboration, including clients, suppliers, universities, and employees. This indicates a need for increased openness, awareness, and structural integration of innovation methods and partnerships.

5.4.4 Internal Capital Over External Aid: Financing Innovation in German Manufacturing Small and Medium-Sized Enterprises

The analysis of financing options for innovation in German manufacturing SMEs, based on the one-sample t-test results shown in Table 5.4, reveals a clear preference for internal funding mechanisms, coupled with a general reluctance or limited use of external financial instruments.

The results show that the most probable source of innovation financing is the reinvestment of profits. Respondents indicate a high likelihood of using this option (mean = 1.51, $p < 0.001$), which is also confirmed by their actual practice (mean = 1.42, $p < 0.001$). In contrast, external financing options are met with considerable hesitation. There is a statistically significant but negative tendency to raise capital (mean = −0.18, $p < 0.001$), take bank loans (mean = −0.26, $p < 0.001$), or use crowdfunding (mean = −0.38, $p < 0.001$) or venture capital (mean = −0.63, $p < 0.001$) to fund innovation.

Actual use of these external instruments is also very limited. The data show that respondents have not raised fresh capital (mean = −1.14, $p < 0.001$), taken bank loans (mean = −0.75, $p < 0.001$), or used crowdfunding (mean = −1.79, $p < 0.001$) or venture capital (mean = −1.62, $p < 0.001$). In addition, they have not made significant use of tax credits (mean = −1.33, $p < 0.001$) or government grants (mean = −0.83, $p < 0.001$), despite a stated likelihood of utilizing tax credits (mean = 0.25, $p < 0.001$) and applying for government grants (mean = 0.50, $p < 0.001$).

Importantly, the perceived administrative burden associated with public funding schemes is a notable barrier. Respondents strongly agree that government-subsidized funding creates excessive overhead (mean = 1.05, $p < 0.001$), which may explain their limited engagement with such programmes in practice.

In summary, German manufacturing SMEs predominantly rely on internal financing through profit reinvestment to support innovation activities. While there is some intention to use tax incentives and public grants, the actual application of these and other external financing instruments remains minimal. Administrative complexity and overheads associated with government funding appear to act as a significant deterrent.

Table 5.4 One-Sample t-Test on financing options for innovation

One-Sample t-Test						
	Test Value = 0					
	t	df	Sig. (2-tailed)	Mean Difference	95% Confidence Interval of the Difference	
					Lower	Upper
Likely to reinvest profits to finance innovation	47.14	370	0.000	1.510	1.45	1.57
Likely to raise capital to finance innovation	−3.07	370	0.000	−0.180	−0.29	−0.06
Likely to take bank loan to finance innovation	−4.44	370	0.000	−0.260	−0.38	−0.15
Likely to seek government grants to finance innovation	8.24	370	0.000	0.500	0.38	0.62
Likely to use tax credits to finance innovation	4.06	370	0.000	0.250	0.13	0.38
Likely to use crowdfunding to finance innovation	−6.38	370	0.000	−0.380	−0.5	−0.26
Likely to use venture capital to finance innovation	−9.81	370	0.000	−0.630	−0.76	−0.51
Have reinvested profits for innovation	27.80	370	0.000	1.420	1.32	1.52
Have raised fresh capital for innovation	−18.69	370	0.000	−1.140	−1.26	−1.02
Have used bank loans for innovation	−11.05	370	0.000	−0.750	−0.88	−0.62
Have used government grants for innovation	−12.60	370	0.000	−0.830	−0.96	−0.7
Have used tax credits for innovation	−25.22	370	0.000	−1.330	−1.43	−1.22
Have used crowdfunding for innovation	−55.73	370	0.000	−1.790	−1.85	−1.73
Have used venture capital for innovation	−31.71	370	0.000	−1.620	−1.71	−1.51
Government-subsidized funding creates too much overhead	21.41	370	0.000	1.050	0.95	1.14

5.4.5 Strategic Safeguarding: Intellectual Property Management and Innovation Protection

The analysis of intellectual property (IP) treatment and innovation protection in German manufacturing SMEs, as presented in Table 5.5, indicates a clear and statistically significant tendency among respondents to actively safeguard their innovations through various formal mechanisms.

The data show that respondents demonstrate a strong inclination to protect new developments through patents (mean = 0.83, $p < 0.001$), registered designs (mean = 0.71, $p < 0.001$), and trademarks (mean = 0.80, $p < 0.001$). These findings highlight a broad strategic approach to formal IP protection, suggesting that SMEs in this sector place high value on securing legal exclusivity for their innovations.

In addition to formal legal instruments, respondents also acknowledge alternative forms of protection (mean = 0.29, $p < 0.001$), which include the strategic use of technical barriers. This may involve the integration of advanced and less accessible production technologies—such as additive manufacturing processes (e.g., moulded interconnect devices, 3D printing)—to make replication by competitors more difficult, as outlined in a prior section.

Furthermore, the use of external knowledge and resources is evident. Respondents report the application of third-party licenses in their innovation activities (mean = 0.19, $p < 0.001$), indicating that open innovation through legally governed

Table 5.5 One-Sample t-Test on IP management and innovation protection

One-Sample t-Test						
	Test Value = 0					
	t	df	Sig. (2-tailed)	Mean Difference	95% Confidence Interval of the Difference	
					Lower	Upper
Protection of new developments by patents	13.73	370	0.000	0.830	0.71	0.95
Protection of new developments by registered design	12.26	370	0.000	0.710	0.6	0.83
Protection of new developments by trademark	13.94	370	0.000	0.800	0.69	0.91
Protection of new developments by other	4.97	370	0.000	0.290	0.18	0.41
Use license from third parties for innovation	4.67	370	0.000	0.190	0.11	0.26

collaboration plays a minor but statistically significant role in their innovation practices.

In summary, German manufacturing SMEs employ a multifaceted IP protection strategy that relies heavily on formal legal protections such as patents, trademarks, and registered designs, supplemented by technological inaccessibility and, to a lesser extent, third-party licensing.

5.4.6 Beyond Patents: KPI-Driven Evaluation of Innovation Success

The analysis of innovation success measurement among German manufacturing SMEs reveals a comprehensive and structured approach to evaluating the outcomes of innovation activities. As shown in Table 5.6, the respondents report a high likelihood of assessing the commercial success of innovations as a standard component of their operations (mean = 0.73, $p < 0.001$). This suggests a widespread institutionalization of innovation evaluation within the sector.

Key performance indicators (KPIs) play a central role in this measurement process. The most prominent KPI identified is the contribution of innovation to turnover (mean = 1.11, $p < 0.001$), indicating a strong emphasis on the financial returns generated through innovative efforts. In addition, SMEs report the use of other KPIs such as the contribution to cost reductions (mean = 0.74, $p < 0.001$), process optimization (mean = 0.78, $p < 0.001$), quality improvements (mean = 0.50, $p < 0.001$), and image enhancements (mean = 0.75, $p < 0.001$). These KPIs highlight a broad perspective on innovation benefits beyond mere profitability, encompassing operational efficiency, product or service quality, and brand reputation.

Further indicators include the influence of innovation on other technologies (mean = 0.26, $p < 0.001$) and on projects (mean = 0.59, $p < 0.001$), suggesting that innovations are evaluated for their wider technological and developmental impact.

The data also indicate that innovation success is systematically integrated into the innovation process itself (mean = 0.68, $p < 0.001$), reinforcing the notion that evaluation is not a one-off activity but a continuous component of innovation management. Importantly, innovation success is reported to have a significant influence on future innovation projects (mean = 0.94, $p < 0.001$) and on broader strategic decisions (mean = 1.08, $p < 0.001$), underlining the strategic relevance of innovation measurement within these firms.

However, despite this broad use of KPIs, the number of registered intellectual property rights (IPRs) is not regarded as an appropriate metric for measuring innovation success (mean = −0.88, $p < 0.001$). This implies that formal IP registration is not considered a core performance criterion, possibly due to the limited direct commercial value or the administrative burden associated with such registrations.

Table 5.6 One-Sample t-Test on innovation success measurement

One-Sample t-Test						
	Test Value = 0					
	t	df	Sig. (2-tailed)	Mean Difference	95% Confidence Interval of the Difference	
					Lower	Upper
Measurement of commercial success of innovation is standard	15.36	370	0.000	0.730	0.63	0.82
KPI number of registered IPRs	−15.60	370	0.000	−0.880	−0.99	−0.77
KPI contribution to turnover	23.45	370	0.000	1.110	1.01	1.2
KPI impact on other technologies	4.56	370	0.000	0.260	0.15	0.38
KPI influences on project	10.86	370	0.000	0.590	0.48	0.7
KPI contribution to cost reductions	13.44	370	0.000	0.740	0.64	0.85
KPI contribution to process optimization	14.41	370	0.000	0.780	0.68	0.89
KPI quality improvements	8.54	370	0.000	0.500	0.38	0.61
KPI image enhancements	13.66	370	0.000	0.750	0.64	0.85
Include measurement of innovation success in innovation process	16.63	370	0.000	0.680	0.6	0.76
Innovation success has an impact on future projects	24.12	370	0.000	0.940	0.86	1.01
Innovation success has an impact on strategic decisions	31.12	370	0.000	1.080	1.01	1.15

In summary, German manufacturing SMEs apply a wide range of commercially and operationally focused KPIs to assess innovation success, which plays a critical role in shaping both project-level execution and long-term strategic direction. However, they largely reject the number of registered IPRs as a meaningful success metric.

5.4.7 Unlocking Strategic and Operational Gains: Perceived Benefits of Open Innovation

The analysis of the perceived advantages and threats associated with the open innovation (OI) approach among German manufacturing SMEs, reveals a predominantly positive assessment of the practical benefits of OI as shown in Table 5.7. Respondents identify several significant advantages of the OI model, particularly in terms of operational efficiency and strategic development.

Table 5.7 One-Sample t-Test on the advantages and threats of the OI approach

One-Sample t-Test						
	Test Value = 0					
	t	df	Sig. (2-tailed)	Mean Difference	95% Confidence Interval of the Difference	
					Lower	Upper
OI is an appropriate approach for the company	0.18	370	0.860	0.010	−0.08	0.1
Reducing development cost is an advantage of OI	9.75	370	0.000	0.470	0.37	0.56
Reducing development time is an advantage of OI	8.89	370	0.000	0.440	0.34	0.53
Technology transfer to companies is an advantage of OI	8.52	370	0.000	0.420	0.32	0.51
Technology transfer to other products is an advantage of OI	8.92	370	0.000	0.430	0.33	0.52
Increasing the company's awareness is an advantage of OI	7.81	370	0.000	0.380	0.28	0.48
Establishment of a new business model is an advantage of OI	9.55	370	0.000	0.470	0.38	0.57

Among the most prominent benefits, reducing development costs is rated highly (mean = 0.47, $p < 0.001$), indicating that firms view OI as a means to optimize R&D expenditures. Similarly, reducing development time is perceived as a significant advantage (mean = 0.44, $p < 0.001$), suggesting that collaboration and external inputs help accelerate innovation cycles.

In addition to time and cost efficiencies, technology transfer is another critical benefit attributed to OI. Respondents recognize the transfer of technology to partner companies (mean = 0.42, $p < 0.001$) and to other products (mean = 0.43, $p < 0.001$) as key enablers of innovation scalability and cross-application, highlighting the capacity of OI to extend the value of technological advancements beyond their initial context.

The data also indicate that OI contributes to broader organizational goals. Increasing company awareness (mean = 0.38, $p < 0.001$) and supporting the establishment of new business models (mean = 0.47, $p < 0.001$) are both considered relevant outcomes of adopting an open innovation strategy. These findings underscore the strategic role of OI not only in improving innovation performance but also in fostering organizational transformation and visibility.

However, despite these recognized benefits, the only statement that does not achieve statistical significance is whether OI is considered an appropriate approach for the company overall (mean = 0.01, $p = 0.860$). This suggests a degree of uncertainty or ambivalence among respondents regarding the overall fit of OI with their specific corporate contexts. While individual advantages are clearly acknowledged, companies may still face structural, cultural, or strategic barriers that limit full alignment with the OI paradigm.

The findings provide a foundation for further segmented analysis, which is addressed in subsequent sub-chapters (5.5 to 5.11) to explore how these perspectives vary across different respondent groups.

5.5 Navigating Innovation in the Mechanical Industry—Strategic Priorities, Cultural Practices, and Cautious Adoption of Open Innovation

The general innovation landscape within the mechanical industry reveals that respondents perceive innovation as crucial for business growth, focusing on both product and process innovation. Their strategic objectives prioritize quality leadership, market leadership, and technology leadership, while they do not engage in business model innovation nor regard factors such as protection rights, import restrictions, customer expectations, regulation, or certification as significant barriers to innovation.

Regarding innovation culture, respondents actively involve production, research and development, and marketing leaders in innovation initiatives, allocate time and financial resources to employees for innovation activities, and communicate innovation successes internally. Nonetheless, they do not encourage employee-driven innovation nor provide dedicated working spaces for such purposes. Familiarity with the concept of open innovation and knowledge management exists, whereas awareness of crowdsourcing, design thinking, market-driven innovation, innovation campus, and the blue ocean strategy is limited. Clients are considered potential innovation partners, whereas competitors, investors, employees, suppliers, research institutions, universities, and development service providers are generally not. Innovation partnerships are primarily formed through recommendations and customer projects. Prior to innovating, respondents conduct market studies and actively seek to influence their partners to meet innovation objectives.

In terms of financing innovation, respondents tend to reinvest profits and pursue government grants but generally avoid crowdfunding and venture capital. They express concerns over the administrative burden associated with government-subsidized funding. Empirically, these firms have not utilized fresh capital, bank loans, crowdfunding, or venture capital for innovation financing, though they are likely to use tax credits.

Intellectual property management is well established, with respondents protecting innovations through patents, registered designs, trademarks, and other mechanisms, including the use of third-party licenses to support innovation efforts.

Measurement of innovation success is integrated as a standard procedure, with key performance indicators (KPIs) focused on turnover contribution, cost reduction, process optimization, image enhancement, project influence, and quality improvement. Innovation success metrics are embedded within the innovation process and significantly impact future projects and strategic company decisions. However, KPIs do not substantially affect other technologies.

Finally, the advantages of the open innovation approach are recognized in reducing development costs and time, facilitating technology transfer both to partner companies and across product lines, enhancing corporate awareness, and supporting the establishment of new business models. Despite these benefits, respondents do not perceive open innovation as an entirely appropriate approach for their companies, indicating a cautious or ambivalent stance towards full adoption of this innovation paradigm.

5.6 Driving Innovation in the Automotive Industry: Strategic Focus, Cultural Practices, and Pragmatic Adoption of Open Innovation

The respondents in the automotive industry focus on both product and process innovation, aiming to achieve leadership in quality, market presence, cost efficiency, technology, and overall competitiveness. They identify customer expectations, certifications, and import restrictions as the primary barriers to innovation.

Regarding innovation culture, key figures from production, R&D, sales, and marketing are actively involved in innovation projects. The companies allocate time and financial resources to support employee innovation efforts and communicate innovation successes internally. However, they neither encourage employee-driven innovation initiatives nor provide dedicated innovation workspaces for employees.

In terms of open innovation, respondents are familiar with concepts such as open innovation, crowdsourcing, design thinking, knowledge management, and market-driven innovation, though they are unaware of the innovation campus and blue ocean method. Despite this awareness, the tools related to design thinking, knowledge management, and market-driven innovation are not employed. Innovation partners are primarily found through recommendations and customer projects rather than innovation networks, technology clusters, or calls for tender. Innovation partners typically include clients, suppliers, investors, companies from other industries, and employees, whereas competitors, research institutions, universities, government, and development service providers are generally excluded.

When it comes to financing innovation, companies tend to reinvest profits into innovation but avoid raising fresh capital or using government grants, tax credits, crowdfunding, bank loans, or venture capital. Government-subsidized funding is viewed as burdensome due to administrative overhead. Additionally, respondents are unlikely to raise capital, take bank loans, or use crowdfunding to support innovation.

Intellectual property management involves protecting innovations through patents, registered designs, and trademarks, while other protective measures and third-party licensing are also utilized.

The measurement of innovation success is standard practice, with KPIs focusing on contribution to turnover, impact on other technologies, influence on projects, cost reduction, and process optimization. Measurement of innovation success is integrated into the innovation process, with outcomes affecting future projects and strategic decisions. However, the number of registered intellectual property rights is not used as a KPI. Instead, quality improvements and company image enhancement are considered important metrics.

Finally, the open innovation approach is viewed positively and deemed appropriate for the automotive companies. Its advantages include reducing development time and costs, facilitating technology transfer to new products and partner companies, increasing corporate awareness, and supporting the creation of new business models.

5.7 Innovation Dynamics in the Healthcare Sector: Strategic Priorities, Cultural Constraints, and Selective Engagement with Open Innovation

Respondents in the healthcare industry engage in both product and process innovation, targeting leadership in quality, cost, market, and technology to maintain competitiveness. They identify import restrictions, customer expectations, regulatory demands, and certification requirements as barriers to innovation, while intellectual property protection is not seen as a significant obstacle.

Regarding innovation culture, key roles such as production and sales heads are involved in innovation activities, whereas R&D and marketing leaders are not. Employees are allocated time and financial resources for innovation, and company innovation successes are communicated internally. However, there is no active promotion of employee-driven innovation initiatives, nor is a dedicated workspace provided for innovation activities.

In the context of open innovation, respondents have familiarity with the concepts of knowledge management and open innovation but are generally unaware of innovation campus, crowdsourcing, design thinking, market-driven innovation, and the blue ocean method. They do not utilize crowdsourcing, innovation campus, blue ocean method, or market-driven innovation tools. Innovation partnerships are formed primarily with competitors, research institutions, investors, development providers, government entities, companies from other industries, and development service providers, while clients, suppliers, universities, and employees are not considered innovation partners. The respondents do not seek to influence their innovation partners to achieve innovation goals and typically identify partners through technology clusters, innovation networks, and calls for tender. Tools such as design thinking and knowledge management are not employed, nor are market studies conducted prior to innovation activities.

Concerning innovation financing, respondents tend to reinvest profits into innovation and have done so historically. Although they consider government-subsidized funding to involve excessive administrative overhead, they have not raised fresh capital, nor used tax credits, crowdfunding, or venture capital. They are likely to pursue government grants and tax credits but unlikely to raise capital through bank loans, crowdfunding, or venture capital.

In terms of intellectual property management, innovations are protected through patents, registered designs, trademarks, and other methods, with third-party licensing also in use.

The measurement of innovation success is an established process within these companies. Key performance indicators (KPIs) focus on contributions to turnover, cost reduction, process optimization, and corporate image enhancement. Innovation success measurement is integrated into the innovation process and influences future projects and strategic decisions. The number of registered intellectual property rights is not considered a suitable KPI. Nonetheless, measurable KPIs include the impact on other technologies, influence on projects, and quality improvements.

Regarding open innovation, healthcare SMEs generally regard the approach as inappropriate for their companies. Nevertheless, they acknowledge its benefits in reducing development time and costs, facilitating technology transfers, enhancing corporate profile, and enabling the establishment of new business models.

5.8 Innovation Practices in the Electrical Industry: Strategic Focus, Cultural Constraints, and Selective Adoption of Open Innovation

Respondents in the electrical industry recognize innovation as crucial for business growth, focusing on product and process innovation with goals of quality, cost, market, and technology leadership. They perceive customer expectations and certification requirements as barriers to innovation, whereas protection rights, regulation, and import restrictions are not seen as obstacles.

In terms of innovation culture, heads of R&D, sales, marketing, and production are involved in innovation activities. Companies allocate time and financial resources for innovation to employees and communicate innovation successes internally. However, employee-driven innovation initiatives are neither promoted nor supported with dedicated workspace.

Regarding open innovation, respondents are familiar with the concepts of open innovation, crowdsourcing, and knowledge management but are not aware of the blue ocean method, innovation campus, design thinking, or market-driven innovation. They do not utilize crowdsourcing, innovation campus, design thinking, or the blue ocean method in practice. Competitors, investors, companies from other industries, government entities, and development service providers are considered appropriate innovation partners, whereas clients, employees, suppliers, research facilities, and universities are not. Prior to innovation, market studies are not conducted, nor do they actively influence their innovation partners to achieve innovation goals. Innovation partners are mainly identified through technology clusters, innovation networks, and calls for tender. Knowledge management tools and market-driven innovation methods are not employed.

In innovation financing, respondents typically reinvest profits into innovation and have done so previously. Government-subsidized funding is viewed as administratively burdensome. Venture capital, fresh capital, tax credits, crowdfunding, and bank loans are generally not utilized for financing innovation, though government grants and tax credits remain potential sources of funding.

Intellectual property management involves protecting innovations through patents, registered designs, trademarks, and other measures, alongside the use of licenses from third parties.

Measuring innovation success is a standardized process, with KPIs focused on contribution to turnover and influence on projects. Innovation success measurement is integrated into the innovation process and affects future projects and strategic decision-making. KPIs such as impact on other technologies, cost reduction, process optimization, quality improvements, and image enhancement are statistically insignificant, and the number of registered intellectual property rights is not used as a success metric.

Finally, the open innovation approach is generally perceived as inappropriate for companies in the electrical industry. Nonetheless, its advantages are recognized in reducing development time and costs, facilitating technology transfer to products and companies, enhancing corporate awareness, and providing opportunities to establish new business models.

5.9 Innovation Dynamics in Software and Computer Services: Strategic Priorities, Cultural Practices and Selective Engagement with Open Innovation

Small and medium-sized enterprises in the software and computer services industry regard innovation as essential for business growth, focusing on product, process, and business model innovation with the goals of quality, market, and technology leadership, but not cost leadership. Customer expectations are perceived as a barrier to innovation, whereas regulation, certification, protection rights, and import restrictions are not considered obstacles.

In terms of innovation culture, these companies involve heads of production, R&D, and marketing in innovation activities, but not the head of sales. They allocate time and financial resources to support innovation among employees and communicate innovation successes internally. However, employee-driven innovation initiatives are not actively promoted, nor is dedicated workspace provided for innovation.

Regarding open innovation, respondents are familiar with the concepts of open innovation, crowdsourcing, and knowledge management, but not with the blue ocean method or innovation campus. Despite some awareness of design thinking and market-driven innovation, these tools are not widely used, and neither are crowdsourcing or the blue ocean method. Innovation partners are typically identified through technology clusters and other channels beyond customer projects. Competitors, investors, and the state are regarded as potential innovation partners, while clients, suppliers, and universities are generally not considered as such. Additionally, research facilities, companies from other industries, and development service providers are seen as possible partners, although these results are statistically insignificant. Market studies are not routinely conducted prior to innovation, nor do companies actively influence their partners to achieve innovation objectives.

In terms of financing, these SMEs tend to reinvest profits into innovation and may seek government-subsidized funds despite perceiving such funding as administratively burdensome. They generally do not take bank loans, raise fresh capital, or use government grants, tax credits, crowdfunding, or venture capital for financing innovation. Although the likelihood of using tax credits is indicated, crowdfunding and venture capital are unlikely sources of funding.

For intellectual property management, respondents protect their innovations through patents, registered designs, trademarks, and other measures, while also utilizing third-party licenses.

Innovation success is measured as a standard procedure, using KPIs such as contribution to turnover, impact on other technologies, influence on projects, cost reduction, process optimization, and image enhancement. The number of registered intellectual property rights is not considered a relevant KPI. Innovation success measurement is integrated into the innovation process and influences future projects and strategic decisions. Quality improvement, however, is statistically an insignificant measure of success.

Regarding the open innovation approach, respondents perceive it as beneficial for reducing development time and costs, facilitating technology transfer to companies and other products, and enabling the establishment of new business models. Nonetheless, they do not consider open innovation an appropriate approach for their companies nor do they believe it enhances their corporate profile.

5.10 Innovation Practices in Manufacturing Companies: Strategic Focus, Cultural Patterns, and Cautious Adoption of Open Innovation

In the manufacturing industry, innovation is regarded as crucial for business growth, with companies primarily focusing on product and process innovation rather than business model innovation. Their strategic aim centers on quality leadership, while cost, market, and technology leadership are not primary objectives. Protection rights and import restrictions are not perceived as barriers to innovation; instead, customer expectations and certification requirements represent the main obstacles.

The innovation culture within these companies involves engaging heads of production, R&D, and marketing in innovation activities, though sales leadership is excluded. Employees are granted time and financial resources to innovate, and innovation successes are communicated internally. However, employee-driven innovation initiatives are neither actively promoted nor supported with dedicated working spaces.

Regarding open innovation, respondents are familiar with the term but lack awareness of specific methods such as innovation campus, blue ocean strategy, market-driven innovation, crowdsourcing, design thinking, and knowledge management. Innovation partners are typically identified through innovation networks, technology clusters, and calls for tender, rather than through recommendations or customer projects. Competitors, investors, the state, and development service providers are recognized as innovation partners, whereas clients, suppliers, and employees are generally excluded. The respondents do not utilize crowdsourcing or other innovation tools mentioned above and typically do not conduct market studies prior to innovation, nor do they actively influence their innovation partners to meet innovation goals. Research facilities, universities, and companies from other industries are not commonly considered innovation partners.

Financially, these companies tend to reinvest profits into innovation and show interest in government grants, though such funding is often seen as administratively burdensome and has not yet been utilized. They generally avoid venture capital, fresh capital raising, tax credits, crowdfunding, and bank loans, although there is some likelihood they would consider bank loans and tax credits.

Intellectual property management involves protecting innovations through patents, registered designs, trademarks, and other methods, including licensing from third parties.

Innovation success is routinely measured using key performance indicators (KPIs) such as contribution to turnover, cost reduction, process optimization, quality improvement, and company image enhancement. The measurement process is integrated into the innovation cycle and informs future projects and strategic decision-making. Additionally, the impact on other technologies and influence on subsequent projects are considered important success metrics.

While respondents acknowledge several advantages of the open innovation approach—such as reducing development time and costs, facilitating technology transfer, enhancing company visibility, and enabling new business models—they do not view open innovation as an appropriate strategy for their companies.

5.11 Cross-Industry Patterns in Innovation Activities: Strategic Priorities, Barriers, and Collaborative Practices

The industry sectors reveal clear patterns in the pursuit of innovation, strategic intentions, barriers and collaboration practices as shown in Table 5.8.

Across all sectors, product and process innovation are widely implemented, whereas business model innovation is less common and limited to a few industries. Quality leadership and maintaining competitiveness are universal strategic intentions, while technology leadership is also frequently targeted, though not consistently across all industries. By contrast, cost leadership and market leadership are pursued only selectively.

Barriers to innovation are unevenly distributed. Customer expectations are seen as an obstacle in several sectors, while regulations and certifications represent sector-specific challenges. However, protection rights and import restrictions are not considered barriers in any industry.

Regarding organizational involvement, R&D and production heads play a central role in most industries, whereas sales and marketing heads are generally not engaged. Firms across all sectors consistently provide employees with time and financial resources for innovation and communicate innovation success internally. However, they do not promote employee-driven innovation initiatives nor do they offer dedicated workspaces for innovation.

Table 5.8 Summary of the quantitative findings by industry sector

Summary of the quantitative findings by industry sector							
Item	All	MI	A.I	HI	EI	SCS	MF
Conduct Product innovation	✔	✔	✔	✔	✔	✔	✔
Conduct Process innovation	✔	✔	✔	✔	?	✔	✔
Conduct Business model innovation	✖	?	?	?	✖	?	✔
Intention is quality leadership	✔	✔	✔	✔	✔	✔	✔
Intention is cost leadership	?	?	✔	?	?	?	?
Intention is market leadership	?	?	✔	?	?	?	?
Intention is technology leadership	✔	✔	✔	?	✔	✔	?
Intention is keeping our competitiveness	✔	✔	✔	✔	✔	✔	✔
Customer expectation is a barrier to innovation	✔	?	✔	?	✔	✔	?
Regulation is a barrier to innovation	✖	✖	?	?	?	✖	✖
Certification is a barrier to innovation	✖	?	?	?	?	✖	✖
Protection right is a barrier to innovation	✖	✖	✖	✖	✖	✖	✖
Import restriction is a barrier to innovation	✖	✖	✖	✖	✖	✖	✖
R&D head is involved in innovation	✔	✔	✔	?	✔	?	?
Sales head is involved in innovation	?	?	?	?	?	?	?
Marketing head is involved in innovation	?	?	?	?	?	?	?
Production head is involved in innovation	✔	✔	✔	✔	✔	✔	✔
Promotion of employees' innovation initiatives	✖	✖	✖	✖	✖	✖	✖
Give innovation workspace to employees	✖	✖	✖	✖	✖	✖	✖
Give time for innovation	✔	✔	✔	✔	✔	✔	✔
Give financial resources to employees	✔	✔	✔	✔	✔	✔	✔
Company's innovation success communicated to employees	✔	✔	✔	✔	✔	✔	✔
Heard the term open innovation	✔	✔	✔	✔	✔	✔	✔
Heard of crowdsourcing	?	✖	?	?	?	✔	?
Heard of innovation campus	✖	✖	?	✖	✖	?	✖
Heard of design thinking	✖	✖	?	?	✖	✔	✖
Heard of knowledge management	?	✖	?	?	?	✔	?
Heard of blue ocean method	✖	✖	✖	✖	✖	✖	✖
Heard of market-driven method	?	?	?	?	?	?	✖
Used crowdsourcing	✖	✖	✖	✖	✖	✖	✖
Used innovation campus	✖	✖	✖	✖	✖	✖	✖
Used design thinking	✖	✖	?	✖	✖	?	✖
Used knowledge management	✖	✖	?	?	✖	✔	✖
Used blue ocean method	✖	✖	✖	✖	✖	✖	✖
Used market-driven method	✖	✖	?	✖	✖	✖	✖

(continued)

Table 5.8 (continued)

Summary of the quantitative findings by industry sector							
Item	All	MI	A.I	HI	EI	SCS	MF
Contribution to innovation work with others	✖	✖	✔	✖	✖	✖	✖
Found partner through innovation networks	✔	✖	?	?	✔	✔	✔
Found partner through technology cluster	✔	✖	?	✔	✔	✔	✔

✔Accepted = Mean value positive and $p < 0.05$; ✖Rejected = Mean value negative and $p < 0.05$; ? Not supported $p > 0.05$
MI = Mechanical industry; A.I. = Automotive industry; HI = Healthcare Industry; EI = Electrical Industry; SCS = Software and Computer services Industry; MF = Manufacturing Industry

Awareness of innovation concepts is widespread, as all industries are familiar with open innovation. Crowdsourcing, knowledge management, design thinking, and market-driven methods are known in selected industries, whereas the blue ocean method and innovation campus are largely unfamiliar. Despite this awareness, actual application remains limited: only a few industries apply design thinking, knowledge management, or market-driven approaches, while crowdsourcing, innovation campuses, and the blue ocean method are not used at all.

Collaboration practices also vary. Some industries actively engage with external partners and find them through innovation networks or technology clusters, while others rely less on structured mechanisms. Contributions to innovation with external partners are selective and more common in certain industries than in others.

In summary, while product and process innovation, quality orientation, and competitiveness are consistently pursued across industries, significant differences exist in strategic focus, barriers encountered, leadership involvement, awareness and use of innovation methods, and collaboration practices.

5.12 Bridging the Gap: Designing Crowdsourcing Platforms for Open Innovation in German Small and Medium-Sized Enterprises

It is obvious that companies understand the value and benefits of Open Innovation, they do not currently use it. The findings also show that these businesses do not use crowdsourcing. Based on these findings as well as the author's proposal experience as the owner manager of an innovative SMEs, the following section analyses presents the outline of a crowdsourcing platform appropriate for Open Innovation by German SMEs.

The crowdsourcing activities are a part of open innovation approach. Open Innovation means that the companies shall open their individual boundaries for third parties to let knowledge come into the company from the outside. Table 5.9 shows an overview of the R&D crowdsourcing platforms.

Table 5.9 Comparison of Research- and development crowdsourcing platforms

Research- and Development platforms	URL	Application	Country	Language	Obstacles for German SMEs to use these platfroms							
					Language	Headquarters	Supporting companies	Industries	IP Protection	Additional provided service	Estimated usage costs for SMEs	Personal online account
InnoCentive	www.innocentive.com	Problem solving scientific-based questions	USA	English	Englisch	Massachusetts, USA	Mainly for multinational enterprises	Pharmaceutical	Lack of confidence in IP protection for German SMEs		35,000$ - 60,000$ (29,969€ - 51,375€)*	Yes
IdeaConnection	www.ideaconnection.com	Idea creation platform	Canada	English	Englisch	Victoria, Canada	N.N	Multiple indsutries	Lack of confidence in IP protection for German SMEs		10,000$ - 100,000$ (8,562€ - 85,626€)*	Yes
Yet2.com	www.yet2.com	Trade patform for copyrights	USA, UK, Japan	English, Japanese	English, Japanese	Massachusetts, USA		Arospace, Medical, Chemical, Agriculture Electrical engineering	Lack of confidence in IP protection for German SMEs		N.A:	No

(continued)

Table 5.9 (continued)

Research- and Development platforms	URL	Application	Country	Language	Obstacles for German SMEs to use these platfroms							
					Language	Headquarters	Supporting companies	Industries	IP Protection	Additional provided service	Estimated usage costs for SMEs	Personal online account
PRESANS	www.presans.com	Problem solving scientific-based questions	France	English	English		Mainly for multinational enterprises	Multiple indsutries			N.A:	No
Hypios	www.hypios-ci.com	Problem solving scientific-based questions	France	French / English	French / English						20,000€ - 35,000€	Yes

(continued)

Table 5.9 (continued)

Research- and Development platforms	URL	Application	Country	Language	Obstacles for German SMEs to use these platfroms							
					Language	Headquarters	Supporting companies	Industries	IP Protection	Additional provided service	Estimated usage costs for SMEs	Personal online account
NineSigma	www.ninesigma.com	Platform for soving technical issues	Japan, Belgium, USA	English	English	Tokyo, Japan	Mainly for multinational enterprises				20,000€ - 50,000€	Yes
Pharma Licensing	www.pharmalicensing.com	Platform for Technology Scouting, Technology Marketing and Government & Education which is related to the pharmaceutical industry	USA, UK	English	English	York, England	Mainly for multinational enterprises	Pharmaceutical			N.A:	Yes

* The cost figures has been converted by the exchange rate from 8th January 2026 by 1 USD – > 0.86€

In the category of R&D crowdsourcing platforms, the platform 'InnoCentive' (Innocentive, 2001) is a large platform which is located in the USA to support multinational enterprises in their crowdsourcing activities, mainly from the pharmaceutical industry. After an online registration by the author, the usage costs could be estimated in accordance to the prizes the participating companies announced for appropriate solutions. Depending on the innovation projects and the size of the innovating company, the monetary compensation the crowdworkers should get for a valuable solution varied from $35,000 to $60,000.

Irrespective of the industry, have difficulties in formulating the individual innovation requirements in English language, so that the needs and requirements cannot be expressed very well on crowdsourcing platforms which operate in English. Most innovation manager responsible for deciding on the implementation of innovation projects in the company and having a corresponding budget, as well as the business owners and corporate executives of traditional German SMEs, though well-educated, have low proficiency in English language. Furthermore, those responsible employees for innovation must properly and clearly communicate with the crowd and the operator of this platform in English language, which is mostly not manageable by the SMEs. Another difficulty is that the platforms are operated in the US and therefore there is a low degree of confidence in the treatment of IP rights towards German companies due to the data protection regulations that apply there. Finally, the high monetary compensation shown above is not affordable for a German SME.

The crowdsourcing platform 'Idea Connection' supports both SMEs and multinational enterprises (Idea Connection, 2007), which might be a positive for this crowdsourcing platform in this context. However, this crowdsourcing platform operates in English language which is a major obstacle for German SMEs. In addition to this, this platform is operated in Canada which presents an IP protection risk for German SMEs. In this case, the sole advantage for German SMES to use this platform is that SMEs too are supported by 'Idea Connection'. However, a difficult hurdle for them is high requisite monetary compensation payable to the crowdworker. The prizes for a valuable solution which the innovating companies displayed, ranged from $10,000 to $100,000. The lower compensation rate might be appropriate for SMEs, which have to be considered case wise.

The crowdsourcing platform Yet2 (Yet2, 1999) was founded in 1999 by multinational enterprises and venture capital companies such as Venrock, 3i, Dupont, Procter & Gamble, Honeywell, Caterpillar, NTT Leasing, Bayer, and Siemens (www.yet2.com/about/history). Beside the traditional crowdsourcing business, this platform offers also innovation consulting, technology scouting, out licensing technology, Open Innovation portals and patent transactions to their clients. This means that this platform offers a holistic service across innovation, patent commercialization and networking activities, which is a major advantage for the innovating companies. Furthermore, projects for companies from various industries such as the aerospace, medical, chemical, agriculture and electrical engineering are implemented, which suggests that this platform as an expert in these fields. As numerous projects from different industries are being worked on, it can be expected that the platform Yet2 support both SMEs and multinational companies in the area of open innovation as well as crowdsourcing and innovation consulting. However, the platform is operated in the English language, which is a major obstacle for traditional German SMEs. In addition to this, the platform 'Yet2' is operated in the USA, which is a further obstacle with regard to the IP protection needs of the German companies due to the data protection regulation.

The crowdsourcing platform 'Presans' was founded in 2008 (Presans, 2008). Beside the traditional crowdsourcing activities, the platform provides a 'up-to-date overview of a field of knowledge, science or technology by leveraging a network' (Presans, 2008) with includes a high number of participants. In addition to this, it also provides innovation strategy guidance to facilitate the evaluation of the company's innovation strategy by a huge network. Such additional service is a great advantage for innovating companies, so that they get a 'soundboard' for their individual needs. An additional advantage is that this platform is operated in France, which has to meet the European General Data Protection Regulation (GDPR), by means they shall treat IP protection rights as per EU standards. This could be a reason for German SMEs to use this platform. Unfortunately, the platform is operated in the English language, which is a major obstacle for traditional German SMEs, as mentioned above.

The crowdsourcing platform 'Hypios' is also located in France (Hypios, 2015), and therefore meets the European General Data Protection Regulation (GDPR) to protect the intellectual property rights, as well as safeguards the additional data of the company from the crowdworker in an appropriate manner. A great advantage of this platform is that it provides an online shop for IP trading of patents and trademarks of multiple industries. This means the platform offers an additional service for innovation and offers patents and other property rights. This way of IP trading might be an additional sales channel for companies to ommercializes their innovations in a short time. Unfortunately, the platform runs in the English language, which is a major obstacle for German SMEs. The prises for a valuable solution, which the innovating companies displayed, differ between €20,000 and €35,000. The lower compensation rate might be applicable for SMEs, which have to be considered case wise. Summarizing this, the mentioned attributes could be a reason for German SMEs to use this platform 'Hypios' for their innovation, except the great obstacle of the English language.

The crowdsourcing platform 'NineSigma' (NineSigma, 2000) was founded in 2000 to solve technical issues for their clients, which are mainly multinational enterprises. This means that they source technology and solution proposals from their innovation community (crowdsourcing) for their clients. In addition to this, the NineSigma-Platform also screens the collected ideas from the crowd to choose the best technology solution in accordance with their clients' requirements. The platform is operated in English language and is located in Japan, Belgium, and USA, which is a major obstacle for German SMEs. But one advantage might be, that the IP treatment, especially by the Belgium subsidiary, shall be based on EU-Legal standards, so that the clients can be assured that their intellectual property rights are protected and particular company secrets are treated confidentially. Given the above-mentioned attributes of this crowdsourcing platform, traditional German SMEs could use this platform, if they engage with the Belgium subsidiary in regard to the IP treatment by EU standards. Furthermore, this platform also provides an additional innovation service. It involves a technology search in accordance to the clients' requirements. The prizes for a valuable solution, which the innovating companies displayed, ranged between €20,000 and €50,000. The lower compensation rate might be applicable for SMEs, which have to be considered case wise. The platform provides an innovation environment that offers global visibility for the external innovation initiatives.

The innovation platform 'Pharma Licensing' (www.pharmalicensing.com) is an online platform on which only pharmaceutical companies, universities, research facilities, charity organizations or private pharmaceutical institutes can trade their patents and other IP rights. The platform provides various options for filtering the requirements after registration. The platform is registered in the USA and is provided in English language.

Crowdsourcing platforms serve a wide range of functions and can be categorized into distinct types depending on their specialized applications, such as marketing and design, freelance services, idea generation, and micro-task execution. Each category targets different business needs, with international platforms offering broader capabilities and German platforms focusing more narrowly, typically catering to small and medium-sized enterprises (SMEs).

Marketing and Design Platforms are primarily used for generating visual identity components like company logos, corporate design, website layout, print material, and T-shirt design. These platforms function as digital marketplaces where companies pose design tasks to a global pool of ommerci who submit proposals in competitive formats. Examples include platforms that run marketing competitions, allow innovation concepts to be publicly challenged, and offer design crowdsourcing for logos, websites, or brand elements. Some platforms operate internationally, while others are based in Germany and communicate in German, offering localized legal and IP protections, which is particularly relevant for traditional German SMEs.

Freelancer Platforms connect businesses with individuals who can perform simple digital tasks such as web research, keywording, transcription, and surveys. These platforms vary from broad-spectrum marketplaces offering a wide range of freelance services—including copywriting and app development—to more specialized solutions targeting algorithm development, technical design, or virtual lead generation. While several leading platforms are based in the USA or Canada and operate in English, Germany hosts its own platforms where tasks are small, often low-cost, and conducted in multiple European languages.

Idea Creation Platforms are geared towards collaborative innovation. They support brainstorming and ideation processes focused on product development, marketing strategies, and future business scenarios. These platforms facilitate mass collaboration and often include innovation communities, contests, and R&D collaborations. They can also function as incubators for licensing and scientific projects. International platforms offer expansive open innovation networks, while German platforms like Jovoto and Innovationskraftwerk contribute by aligning innovation with local regulatory standards and cultural expectations. These platforms also include socio-political and scientific problem-solving alongside commercial goals.

German-Specific Platforms differ in their limited scope when compared to international counterparts. They tend to concentrate on micro-tasking, which includes online activities such as text writing, translations, web keywording, and content generation for e-commerce. Marketplace platforms provide SEO-optimized content, blogging, and web text production. Design platforms in Germany cover logo and web design services, while testing platforms offer product and software usability testing, accessibility testing, and quality assurance services for digital tools and consumer electronics. Innovation platforms in Germany, though fewer in number, offer structured collaboration models and mass ideation, often with a focus on both business and societal value creation.

One of the major advantages for German SMEs in using domestic crowdsourcing platforms is that these are aligned with German and European legal norms, especially in the areas of data protection and intellectual property (IP). Moreover, German platforms often operate in both German and English, enhancing usability for domestic firms with international reach. These platforms are typically built to serve both SMEs and multinational corporations, meaning that SMEs can indirectly benefit from methodologies and innovations tested with larger clients.

Despite these benefits, it is evident that Germany hosts significantly fewer R&D-oriented crowdsourcing platforms compared to global offerings. Moreover, the existing German platforms do not yet fully embrace the broader range of services and innovation strategies offered by international platforms. This gap presents an opportunity for the development of a tailored crowdsourcing platform specifically designed to meet the complex, quality-focused, and regulation-sensitive needs of traditional German SMEs.

5.13 The Target Product Profile Analysis for a New Crowdsourcing Concept

The target product profile serves as a strategic tool for defining the core characteristics of a newly developed product. Within the framework of the crowdsourcing platform, the minimum requirements of the existing solution were previously examined and, at the same time, the proposed feature set for a new crowdsourcing concept was presented, designed to improve functionality and meet the specific needs of SMEs. For the sake of simplicity, we will omit the full elaboration of the target product profile at this point, but focus on the corresponding analysis results instead.

The existing platforms, as shown previously, operate exclusively in English, whereas the new concept aims to support both German and English, thereby broadening its accessibility for German-speaking users. Intellectual property (IP) protection for both solution seekers and crowdworkers is currently aligned with European law; in contrast, the new model proposes legal compliance tailored specifically to German legislation, providing more locally relevant legal safeguards.

Data protection remains consistent in both models, adhering to European Union regulations. However, the new concept introduces a formal quality management system in line with ISO 9001:2015 standards, which is currently absent in the existing platform.

Accessibility of the platform in its current form is limited to a web-based interface. The new concept expands this by including mobile applications compatible with iOS and Android, thereby increasing user flexibility. While the current platform only encrypts and displays the company name of users, the enhanced model offers greater transparency and traceability through the display of both the company and the employee's name.

Additional services form a significant component of the improved crowdsourcing concept. These include consulting services to support innovation process implementation and adjustments, as well as technology scouting combined with foresight capabilities. Moreover, the new concept introduces a structured mechanism for identifying suitable innovation partners—not only among SMEs, but also within the research community.

In terms of financing, the new model proposes an added value service for locating relevant R&D funding programmes and providing support throughout the application process, which is not offered in the current system. Patent trade is retained as a feature, but is expanded to include sub-licensing options, enhancing IP commercialization opportunities.

Both platforms allow for the execution of hackathons. However, the new model modifies the existing invoicing approach for SMEs: while retaining a low monthly subscription fee, it introduces a variable service fee based on additional support provided.

Collectively, these enhancements are designed to align the crowdsourcing platform more closely with the specific legal, operational, and strategic needs of SMEs, thereby increasing usability, compliance, and innovation potential.

5.14 A Concept for a New Crowdsourcing Platform and Its Unique Selling Points

As described earlier, the notion of innovation is very important for the German SMEs. Many companies have declared innovation as a key corporate objective, which they consider vital for the growth of a company and its economic success. The surveys have also revealed that companies do not follow a structured innovation process. This sub-chapter shall introduce the general requirements of a new crowdsourcing platform which should lead to potential business success for German SMEs.

5.14.1 General Requirements to the New Future Platform

As shown previously, most of the crowdsourcing platforms which are dealing with Research- and Development issues are not located in Germany. These are located in USA, Canada, Japan, or Belgium. None of the above-mentioned crowdsourcing platforms which deal with the R&D is located in Germany and therefore are not suitable for the traditional German SMEs. This also means that they operate through English language. As described above, from personal and professional experience of the author, the most innovation managers and relevant people for R&D activities in SMEs have significant difficulties to formulate the requirements of an innovation project in English language, because of their age, education and skills. For that reason, a new crowdsourcing platform for German SMEs have to set up in German language. In this situation, the German language limits the scope of such platform to Germany, parts of Switzerland, Austria as well as the eastern part of the Netherlands. For this reason, it is equally important to offer this new platform in English language, to give the innovating companies the option to expand their individual innovation to other nations. However, this requires that the innovation managers and R&D managers have the capability to formulate the requirements of the innovation project in English language and communicate with the crowd. Depending on the innovation project and the skills of those responsible for innovation, the innovative companies can thus adjust the scope for the individual innovation projects, as companies thereby reach a larger crowd in other countries as well. At this stage, the SMEs can decide whether they conduct a crowdsourcing campaign in the German language or in the English language.

In addition to this, a new crowdsourcing platform should be listed in Germany, and function according to German law. This is important, since both the data protection of the information, the data exchanged and the treatment of property rights must be treated in accordance to the German law. This means that all information exchanged between the crowd and the innovating company must be treated discreetly according to the General Data Protection Regulation (GDPR) principles. Furthermore, IP rights must also be treated according to German law, both for the crowd as well as the innovating companies. Both sides must be provided with a transparent and valid legal framework to register and exploit potential IP rights for both sides in a profitable manner. To ensure these points, the new crowdsourcing platform has to be listed and operated in Germany. If doing so, both the crowd and the innovating companies will have the security of finding a valid and reliable legal framework for the treatment of corporate secrets and property rights. This ensures that the intellectual property of the crowd or of the company is not misused or trade secrets betrayed. Thus, the innovating companies have the certainty that all 'safety-relevant' information for an innovation project that has to be exchanged between the innovation partners in an innovation project does not leave the 'innovation consortium'.

Security, reliability and secure communication between the crowd and the innovating companies via the intermediate platform are crucial in the development environment. For this reason, the companies must firstly receive a secure (in terms of technical security) access and registration process on the platform. An additional point has to be considered here. In the event that a competitor of an innovating company is also active on the new crowdsourcing platform, unless safeguards are in place, much of the information could flow to this competitive company. This must be avoided, otherwise the R&D advantage and the associated competitive advantage would be lost. For this reason, the name of the innovating company must be acronymic encoded at the so-called front end of the crowdsourcing platform. If necessary, it should be presented in a changing manner each time. The crowd and the innovating companies are protected to some extent from the outflow of sensitive R&D data, product information, market information or new technological developments in this way 'encrypted' representation of the company's name.

The users should be given the assurance that both the creation process of a user account and the exchange of information and data, the communication between the crowdsourcing partners in terms of security requirements has been implemented by the platform operators. It is useful to certify the platform by an appropriate certification label. This certification should reflect both the secure payment processes and should document that the exchange and handling of sensitive project data and company data are consistent with the General Protected Data Regulation (GPDR). Such certification can be carried out via a corresponding quality management system according to DIN EN ISO 9001:2015. Both relevant quality requirements in accordance with the quality standard of DIN EN ISO 9001:2015 for the crowdsourcing platform itself can be mapped. Furthermore, corresponding process-certification should be considered which are responsible for the safe handling of sensitive company data and the overall project. The presentation of such quality certifications via a corresponding label on the crowdsourcing platform assures the user of the responsible and secure handling of the corresponding data. As mentioned above, the simple and quick technical access to the crowdsourcing platform is an important criterion so that the platform could be used by both the crowd and the innovating companies in terms of the competitive platforms. This access can be realized via a web-based browsing interface, accessible via the common mobile devices. In addition, it is important to provide the most important functions for the users by an App for mobile devices such as IOS, Android, or Embedded Windows. These easy access paths and an App for mobile devices increase user acceptance. Such access enables fast communication between the innovating companies and the crowd. Furthermore, the companies should give feedback to the crowd in a short time manner on the proposed solution and to build and maintain the necessary permanent contact with the crowd, moreover, the new crowdsourcing platform should provide a chat room in which the crowd (single or multiple user) can interact with the innovating company in a secure, quick and reliable atmosphere to interchange ideas.

5.14.2 Importance 'Innovation' for the New Future Platform

As can be seen from the findings of the qualitative interviews and quantitative survey, the issue of innovation is of importance to all surveyed companies to some extent. Companies link innovation to the business success and to the business growth of the company. For this reason, in addition to the actual crowdsourcing activity, the new crowdsourcing platform should also provide technology scouting, such as the structured observation and the early recognition of changes, potentials and relevant knowledge of technological developments and processes. Furthermore, the new platform should also work as a source of ideas as well as a generator for new ideas on topics relevant to the innovative companies. These further offers represent so-called additional offers for the innovating companies and increases on the one hand the attention as well as the acceptance with the users. The new platform should also offer innovation process consulting as an additional service for innovation-minded SMEs, to provide SMEs with a process-based support for the introduction of an innovation tools namely crowdsourcing. This will be crucial for the SMEs that are taking advantage of crowdsourcing for the first time. This is so, because the introduction of an innovation tool always brings about an adaptation of existing processes as well as existing resources in the innovating company. For this reason, process consulting for SMEs who have no experience with crowdsourcing can be another valuable additional benefit. Another valuable additional benefit might be a so-called match-making programme to access to suitable project partners for cooperation projects as well as government-funded R&D activities by the new platform. In addition, in this context, it should also be possible to prepare the corresponding funding applications for the relevant funding programmes in cooperation with the partners via the platform operator. Furthermore, the consulting of the cooperation partners with regard to the application process, the call-up process and all other activities in a government-funded R&D project is to be offered via the new platform. Thus, an innovation-minded SME will have another opportunity to initiate innovation through funding programmes, if this SME has not yet gained experience with such R&D funding programmes. Another additional benefit of the new crowdsourcing platform will be that companies will be able to offer corresponding intellectual property rights or patents for sale or use on the platform. Thus, the opportunity would be created ommercializesze quickly new innovations and inventions to some extent.

5.14.3 Innovation Culture Shall Be Supported By the New Crowdsourcing Platform

Innovation culture is a further important topic for innovating SMEs as the interviews and the online survey revealed. In the innovation context, the employer-involvement as well as the involvement of necessary departments in a company plays a prominent role in building the innovation culture for the SMEs. For this reason, the new platform has to provide multiple access for users from several departments of one company. This means that the platform has to allow access from different user from one company within one company account. At this stage, it has to be stated that multiple accesses have to be managed by the App. With the multiple accesses for several employees for one company account the requirements of the SMEs in regards of the involving of different stakeholder for one innovation project is met. In addition to this, the new crowdsourcing platform shall contain a so-called marketplace on which already executed projects should be displayed to give interesting insights to the crowd as well as to possible new innovation-willing companies. Furthermore, the marketplace would also highlight which type of industries the platform has already supported. In conclusion this would encourage the crowd to communicate it to their individual community to enhance the acceptance of the platform to new crowds which have been previously described as the 'networking effect'.

5.14.4 Commercialization of Innovations Should Be Supported from the New Crowdsourcing Platform

An additional important topic for the interviewed and surveyed SMEs was the commercialization of their innovations, patents, and other intellectual property rights. But firstly, both the crowd and the companies expect a serious treatment of the individual IP rights, which is the basis of a trusted cooperation. A serious treatment of IP rights means that the crowd scrutinizes its problem-solving proposals by third-party IP rights, because the crowd have to keep the company free from third-party IP rights, on one hand side. On the other side, the companies have to guarantee that the crowd monetarily benefit from its individual issue solving proposal if the company integrate to into their R&D activities. Such IP rights treatments shall be based on German IP protection law. In this situation, the new platform has to provide and communicate explicitly such legal framework to enhance the trust for all participants in an innovation project. To quommercialize-salize the innovations or the intellectual property rights, the companies shall have the option to offer their new technologies, products, services, or property rights which have been created on the new platform by an appropriate marketplace. On this marketplace, the platform should display offers from the companies which are willing to sell their innovations or should offer licenses based on their property rights to other companies. Such marketplace would support the SMEs to commercialize their innovations or their property rights in a short time which was also an important issue identified by this research.

5.14.5 Financing of Innovation Should Be Supported by the New Crowdsourcing Platform

As mentioned above, the financing of innovations is always an important issue for the SMEs, because on the one hand they have limited financial resources for innovation projects in comparison to multinational enterprises. On the other hand, the SMEs have less access to financing options such as bank loans. For this reason, the innovating SMEs could be supported in financing innovation projects by government-granted funds for instance. As also mentioned above, the German government supports the innovating companies in innovation financing through government-granted funds, which are provided for multiple topics, for multiple industries and for multiple project consortia. This means that the German government provides annually a certain amount of money for innovation projects. Such funds are to be applied for in a specific process which is, depending on the project provider or depending on the topic, are highly complex and time-consuming. For this reason, the new platform should provide on the one hand the access to several financial government funds and on the other hand the platform shall also provide advice to the innovating SMEs in the apply process for specific grants. In addition to this the platform shall also give hints to the innovating companies which innovation network could support the company in applying for Government grants and which innovation network could help the innovating company to contact other possible cooperation-willing companies to conduct a cooperative Government-granted innovation project. In addition to this, the innovation costs are always an issue for innovating SMEs. For this reason, the crowdsourcing option should not be very expensive for the companies to use. Different invoicing models could be provided to the innovating companies, because the project management and the project management structure in a company require a stable calculation base for a project and thus the development costs of a product should not become higher than planned. To do justice to the project management with regard to the cost transparency, all costs must be able to be transparently mapped in the project management of the company. This means that the company should not face hidden costs during the crowdsourcing process. Furthermore, the usage costs must not be very high to not jeopardize the overall budget of a development. For this reason, the usage costs, the invoicing model and the transparent presentation of overall costs incurred would play a major role. A user-friendly invoicing model shall be offered from the platform to the innovating companies, which allows the companies to pay a small monthly amount continuously over a long time period of time to enable and engage the companies to use the platform continuously, similar to a subscription model. Such invoicing model benefits the company as it has the advantage that the running costs for using the platform are very low, so that the burden of these costs in the overall cost analysis of a company is low and it represents a low-threshold offer for SMEs. The additional services which are provided from the platform should be separately charged.

5.15 Tailored Crowdsourcing for German Manufacturing Small and Medium-Sized Enterprises: Enhancing Open Innovation, Knowledge Access, and Competitiveness

As seen in the summary of the quantitative findings by industry sector and by company size, most of the surveyed companies conduct R&D projects to develop new products or to improve their existing processes. Their intention for these R&D projects is quality leadership and technology leadership. These companies collaborate with several internal and external stakeholders. Internally it involves mainly the R&D head and production head. The company management also provide time and financial resources to their employees for innovation activities. The survey also revealed that the SMEs do not pursue a structured innovation process, but they have heard of the term 'open innovation'. The involvement of external stakeholders provides access to new knowledge and high calibre research. The surveyed SMEs found external partners through innovation networks, technology clusters or through calls for tender. However, the surveyed SMEs have limited access to universities, research facilities or other companies in their industries. From a financial perspective, the surveyed SMEs reinvest their own profits and government subsidies for innovation. All surveyed SMEs emphasized that this use of government-granted funds creates too much overhead and the relevant mechanisms are not properly designed for usage by SMEs. Finally, the surveyed SMEs see benefit in using open innovation as it has the potential to reduce development time and development costs, through the technology transfer between companies or through the establishment of a new business model. This shows that the open innovation approach is pursued by the surveyed SMEs to some extent but does not give the impression of its use being well-designed or well-structured. For this reason, a new crowdsourcing tool as part of the overall open innovation approach has been suggested to gain access to the external research knowledge, other companies and other innovation stakeholders. As shown earlier, there are numerous crowdsourcing platforms available online, of which, very few are designed for manufacturing SMEs. For this reason, a new crowdsourcing platform, which takes into account the specific demands and requirements of German manufacturing SMEs, has been suggested. This new platform first considers the German location and therewith the German language, as well as the German GDPR and IP laws, which are all important in building trust between the crowdworkers and the German SMEs as crowdsourcer. It also provides German SMEs specific additional services such as technology scouting, technology foresight, a matchmaking provision to find an appropriate innovation partner, a marketplace for IP trading and an SME-friendly billing model to overcome SMEs natural constraints and is designed to help them improve their innovativeness and competitiveness.

References

European Commission. (2016). EU Industrial R&D Investment Scoreboard. Retrieved from http://iri.jrc.ec.europa.eu/scoreboard16.html#modal-two
Hypios. (2015). Hypios-Crowdsourcing platform. Retrieved from www.hypios-ci.com
Idea Connection. (2007). Idea connection—Crowdsourcing platform. Retrieved from www.ideaconnection.com/
Innocentive. (2001). Innocentive—Crowdsourcing platform. Retrieved from www.innocentive.com
NineSigma. (2000). NineSigma—Crowdsourcing platform. Retrieved from www.ninesigma.com
Presans. (2008). Presans—Crowdsourcing platform. Retrieved from www.presans.com
Yet2. (1999). Yet2—Crowdsourcing platform. Retrieved from www.yet2.com/

6 German Small and Medium Enterprises: Harnessing Open Innovation and Crowdsourcing to Sustain Growth

The German economy is well known for its competitive strength. SMEs dominate the German manufacturing landscape far more than they do in any other economy of this size and are often hailed as the 'Hidden Champions' (Simon, 2007). This is because German SMEs make a significant contribution to the growth of the German economy both in output and employment. However, the basic economic outlook for SMEs in Germany is worsening because, on the one hand, taxes are rising, production costs are rising steadily, and the education of potential employees does not meet SMEs' requirements. On the other hand, German SMEs have to deal with the increasingly stiff competition from businesses in emerging markets. In addition to this, the German economy has lost ground in its innovativeness in comparison to other EU member states as well as with other countries in the world as shown above. It is now widely understood that German SMEs can only succeed economically by generating business growth based on innovation. They have to create new products through product innovation, they have to improve their processes through process innovation and they have to invent new business models such as service models (smart services) that enable them to earn money from solely beyond product sales. Their ability to achieve success in these three fields of innovation is possible only if German students are well-educated from school levels up to the universities. SME must adapt to the new competitive conditions as well as utilize new business models. However, the quality of training imparted in schools and universities continues to be bad and the required skills are not demonstrated by the potential employees. This is surprising since Germany has numerous well-regarded universities in pure as well as applied science as described above. For this reason, the SMEs have to further train their new employees to inculcate a sense of the new products, new processes and new business models on the job to perform the innovation. However, this presupposes that companies can hire employees with requisite qualifications. That is the core

M. Vathauer, *Breaking Barriers with Open Innovation in Germany*, Management for Professionals, https://doi.org/10.1007/978-3-032-14660-1_6

issue for SMEs. The experienced employees demand higher salaries, especially in the fields of software engineering, hardware engineering, ICT and in other areas related to the currently bourgeoning digitization phenomenon. This development has become noticeable in Germany in recent years, as the labour unions have demanded ever higher salaries for employees in multinational companies, without considering the needs and requirements of the SMEs. This now means for the SMEs that they have to pay very high salaries for employees just to get them. This means that the profits cannot be reinvested into innovation projects, as much of the earned profits go away as increased employee salaries and incentives, as well as on further increases in corporate taxes and social insurance. In addition, companies in Germany have to pay the highest electricity costs in the European comparison. All this means that German SMEs can invest little money in their innovation projects. That is the reason why the numerous Government-subsidized innovation programmes are of immense value for German SMEs. With the establishment of so-called Leading-Edge Clusters, SMEs will be given a framework to carry out cooperative innovation projects in collaboration with research institutions and other companies. These allow the SMEs to refinance a certain part of the incurred R&D costs. As the in-depth interviews and the online survey carried out for this research show, SMEs have experience in using Government-funded R&D projects to some extent. At the same time, the interviewed and surveyed SMEs claim that the Government-subsidized funds are creating too much overhead. By carrying out cooperative innovation projects in collaboration with research institutions or other companies the innovating SMEs seek to become technology leaders in their particular market field to maintain their current market position. This research also shows that these SMEs have a very close relationship with their customers. This means that sales representatives know exactly the needs and requirements of their customers. Furthermore, because of their flat hierarchies, SMEs can respond more quickly to changes and requirements than multinational enterprises. As a result, SMEs are able to meet the needs of their customers more quickly by offering customized solutions. On the one hand, this approach has the advantage that the SME can generate a strong bond with its customer. On the other hand, company growth is limited accordingly, because of the limited market scope of the individual customer's solutions. That means that business growth is limited due to the limited market size of individual customer solutions, and that the solution created specifically for one or a group of customers cannot be widely deployed on the market, such as a standard solution that can be used by many users and market participants. Due to the customized solution for the customer, the number of customers is limited accordingly and therefore also the company's growth. However, the generated business growth is very sustainable and secure due to great customer loyalty. This means, on the one hand, that innovation can compensate the competitive disadvantages of an SME and, on the other, it can also provide for business growth. The importance of such stakeholder involvement, particularly that of customers, is key to their success in their open innovation. Other stakeholders involved are the suppliers or the employees from different departments such as production, sales, or R&D. The involvement of such stakeholders differs from one innovation project to another. This so-called knowledge management within an overarching open innovation approach drives innovation alongside the company's innovation strategy.

Contrary to a widely held belief, just a few years ago, in SMEs, both strategic decisions and product-specific decisions were solely taken by the business owner or the managing director. This is no longer true in German SMEs. Due to the increasing managerial complexity imposed by market requirements, technical requirements and customer requirements, a single person can no longer make such decisions alone. Such decisions must be taken by a team that has to comprise the managers from different company divisions. For this reason, the open innovation approach fits very well with the needs of German SMEs. Open innovation (OI) involves opening the company's boundaries and gaining new knowledge through the integration of other stakeholders in the company. The open innovation approach is well known in the innovation strategies of multinational companies such as General Electric, Shell or Citrix. These companies have built up a so-called open innovation ecosystem over the last few years, which allows them to apply some of the OI tools. But it is understandable that SMEs cannot build up such a sophisticated OI ecosystem to perform innovation due to their lack of requisite human and financial resources.

SMEs need smart innovation support tailored to the SMEs' requirements. This innovation support has to map the influencing factors, which have an impact on the innovation of an SME, in the sense of SME needs to support innovation and thus innovation success. In the sense of the OI approach, a suitable crowdsourcing platform might be an appropriate innovation tool for SMEs, if such platform meets their requirements. Most SMEs integrate the requisite internal and external stakeholders into their individual innovation. This perspective gives the impression that a crowdsourcing strategy for innovative SMEs is appropriate to support their innovation. Crowdsourcing allows SMEs to involve internal and external stakeholders such as employees from different departments, researchers from universities and research institutes, customers and suppliers. Unfortunately, the evaluations of existing crowdsourcing platforms as shown in Appendix A.14 show that the majority of the technology-driven platforms are located abroad, or they do not meet the German SMEs' specific requirements. For instance, SME-relevant topics are not listed on these platforms. This also means that German SMEs are averse to using such platforms. Further, Germany's crowdsourcing platforms do not address technology-related issues and are therefore of no use to innovation-seeking German SMEs. The next chapter shows how an appropriate crowdsourcing platform could be designed to address the innovation requirements of German SMEs.

6.1 Tailored Crowdsourcing for German Small and Medium-Sized Enterprises: A Comprehensive Platform to Enable Open Innovation

Given the intensifying global competition with companies trying to out-innovate one another (Vyas, 2005, pp. 103–116), it is very difficult for SMEs to achieve significant business growth. On the one hand, companies can buy other companies to gain further market share or to obtain new technologies; the strategy is generally deployed by the multinational corporations. The strategy of buying companies is also observed to some extent in larger non-MNC companies. Involving multiple complex steps, this strategy is very time- and money-consuming, often beyond the calibre of a traditional SME. Another strategy for generating business growth is innovation. Due to increasingly discerning customers and the increasing complexity of technologies, an SME can only carry out successful innovation with the help of appropriate partners. Furthermore, an SME must also involve other stakeholders in their innovation projects, as for both the financing of the innovation and the implementation of the individual project phases, stakeholder participation and commitment is a must. The involvement of project partners also means that the company's natural boundaries must be opened up to third parties. If an SME chooses to open these borders to external third parties, it has a good chance to successfully adopt the open innovation approach. They should also be willing and able to use other requisite tools as shown, including the crowdsourcing platforms. Unfortunately, as discussed above, traditional German SMEs have specific crowdsourcing needs because of their unique traditions and structure and the available crowdsourcing platforms do not meet these needs.

The conceptual foundation for a new crowdsourcing platform tailored to the needs of German small and medium-sized enterprises (SMEs) is derived from the research findings and articulated through a comparative analysis of key platform features. This analysis contrasts the existing functionality of a known international platform with the proposed specifications for a new, locally adapted platform design.

The new crowdsourcing platform is intended to operate bilingually in German and English, in contrast to the existing platform which supports English only. Legal frameworks for intellectual property protection are redefined to reflect German law, providing a more jurisdictionally aligned level of protection for both SMEs and crowdworkers, whereas the existing system adheres only to broader European standards. General data protection remains consistent with European Union regulations across both platforms.

To enhance operational quality, the new platform incorporates a certified quality management system aligned with ISO 9001:2015, which is not present in the existing solution. Accessibility is also significantly improved, expanding from a purely web-based model to include mobile applications compatible with iOS and Android operating systems, thus increasing user reach and engagement.

In terms of data security and user transparency, the current system allows only for the encrypted presentation of the company name. The new concept extends this by including both the company and individual employee names, ensuring greater accountability and traceability in innovation interactions.

Several functional enhancements are introduced to support the innovation lifecycle more comprehensively. These include professional consulting services to assist SMEs in both implementing and refining their innovation processes, and the integration of technology scouting and foresight activities to better anticipate and respond to emerging trends. Additionally, the new platform facilitates the identification of appropriate innovation partners, encompassing both SMEs and research institutions, thereby fostering stronger collaborative networks.

A key advancement is the inclusion of services to help SMEs locate and apply for relevant R&D funding opportunities, supporting financial accessibility for innovation projects. The platform's existing feature of patent trading is retained, but expanded to include sub-licensing mechanisms, broadening options for intellectual property commercialization.

Hackathons remain a strategic element in both models. However, the financial structure for SMEs is revised in the new concept: while maintaining a low monthly subscription fee, it introduces an additional service-based fee model, allowing for more tailored and scalable support.

In summary, the proposed crowdsourcing platform reflects a comprehensive reconfiguration of features designed to meet the legal, technical, and strategic needs of German SMEs, significantly expanding the scope and utility beyond the capabilities of existing platforms.

6.1.1 Designing Crowdsourcing Platforms for German Small and Medium-Sized Enterprises

German SMEs are usually owner-managed and different family members are part of the management team. In this environment, social, ethical political values and business practices play a key role. These values reflect a certain conservatism in German manufacturing SMEs. This conservatism is also reflected in their approach to how they conduct innovation projects. This means that the innovation managers examine very closely which innovation project is initiated, with which partner the SME could run the project, and according to which rules the innovation project is implemented. As a result, features, customer experience, availability and access to the platform, as well as other services that generate additional value for the companies that a business can leverage play a critical role in the success or failure of a new platform.

Furthermore, business-related decisions regarding the company's orientation, corporate strategy and mission are usually taken from the founding generation. Given that the education of the founding generation is not comparable to the current education of today's graduates—which has become very international—the business correspondence language in Germany is German, which also extends to all other business partners such as customers, suppliers, or project partners. One of the findings from the in-depth interviews is that the current innovation managers in SMEs mainly implement local, regional or national innovation projects. The regionality and locality of innovation projects also has the advantage that all project partners involved can be reached quickly by covering short distances to run the innovation project appropriately. From this point of view a new crowdsourcing platform should be designed predominantly for such communication and linguistic requirements. This strongly means that for the platform to gain acceptance among SMEs, the German language must be the medium of exchange on the platform between SMEs and the 'crowd' as well as with the other stakeholders. The advantage is that the innovation managers and the innovation decision makers in an SME have no barrier to entry to the new platform and they have less aversion to its use. Nevertheless, it is necessary to offer a second correspondence language (i.e. English) on the new crowdsourcing platform. This second correspondence language has the advantage that on one hand the scope of influence for the users (the SMEs) is increased and on the other hand a larger stakeholder circle can be involved in the innovation projects. Depending on the SMEs' preferences and the project requirements, only German-speaking or German- and English-speaking project participants can be involved. However, this also means that if an SME has decided to use one or both languages, the crowd will be filtered by the platform according to that language selection, so that the SME acquires a crowd made up of either the German-speaking people or of people with international orientation, too.

6.1.2 Intellectual Property Rights Treatment

The German language as the main correspondence language implies that the platform will also work according to German legal framework conditions. This means that all information exchanged via this new crowdsourcing platform will be handled according to both German legislation and the General Data Protection Regulation (GDPR). For the participating SMEs as well as for the crowd, it is important that confidential company information in particular is handled with care, that project information and new product information does not leave the circle of project participants and that intellectual property rights are protected on the platform under German patent laws and copyright law to ensure the greatest possible security of data protection and know-how protection for SMEs and for the crowd. It is crucial from the perspective of SMEs that sensible project-specific company data does not go beyond the project participants. On the other hand, it is also important for the crowd that the proposed solutions be financially rewarded if they are included in an SME R&D project. The crowd needs the greatest possible certainty from the SMEs that the suggested solutions will be appropriately rewarded when used by the SMEs. This security can only come through appropriate regulation of the new crowdsourcing platform. Thus, in the terms of use, in the general terms and conditions, in the content field of the platform and in all other marketing activities such safeguards must be incorporated.

6.1.3 Encrypted Names of the Employees and Company Name at the Front End

The confidentiality of all activities does not just end with the confidential treatment of company and project data. In some industries, it is also necessary to keep the participating SMEs' names and their employee names confidential. Due to ever-increasing networking in social media as well as the increasing exposure through fairs, exhibitions and internet presentations, well-informed employees of a competitor company can scrutinize the correspondence between the SME and the crowd to discover the topics on which the SME is currently working. To eliminate this vulnerability, the new crowdsourcing platform must, if necessary, present the SME names and corresponding employee names in the so-called front end of the platform in an encrypted manner. This provision serves to increase the confidentiality of the information exchanged between the project partners. At the same time, it also increases the platform's acceptance among innovating SMEs. To further increase acceptance and credibility, this encryption technology must be permanently available to all project participants.

6.1.4 Quality Management System ISO 9001:2015

The new crowdsourcing concept not only includes collaborations between SMEs and the crowd. The new concept also includes the additional crowdsourcing platform offering additional services and services that offer added value for innovative companies. To ensure a high-quality standard for consulting services, technology scouting and IP trading for both the company and the crowd, the new crowdsourcing platform should have a minimum quality standard. The minimum quality standard is documented in German companies via a so-called Quality Management System (QMS) and is certified at regular intervals by a testing centre. The QMS is regulated by a standard, the DIN EN ISO 9001:2015, for which all German companies have to follow a certified QMS. According to DIN EN ISO 9001:2015, quality is the degree of fulfilment of given requirements. ISO 9001:2015 specifies the minimum standard for the QMS that has to be achieved to meet customer requirements and other demands on the product or service quality. The QMS ensures that the platform provider increases the transparency of all business processes, improves sustainable customer satisfaction and significantly lowers the failure rate and the costs. An essential principle of ISO 9001 is the process-oriented approach. A process-oriented QMS documents all essential operational processes and puts them to the test. As a result, optimization opportunities can be revealed even in otherwise well-functioning organizations. The QMS is therefore a factor that interacts intensively with the competitive situation and performance of a provider. A QMS suggests to the clients—in this case both an SME and the crowd—that the platform provider carries out the activities on the platform in a structured manner. This means that in the case of additional consulting services, for instance, the crowdsourcing platform consults SMEs according to a certified process of the

ISO 9001:2015 standard. Furthermore, there is the certainty for the SMEs that the offered service is of a qualified and approved standard. This is guaranteed because all quality-relevant processes are documented in a QMS manual. This means that the awareness of quality is also promoted and internalized by the codification of action in a QMS manual, which is important for both the customer and for new employees of the platform.

6.1.5 Multiple Access to the Platform

As previously mentioned, the crowd expects timely feedback on the submitted innovation proposals from the innovating SMEs. This means that the crowd would like to discuss the suggestions with the responsible innovation manager. Furthermore, the crowd would like to integrate the innovation proposals into the SME's R&D process, if possible, and to be able to access the platform safely at any time and at any opportunity. For this reason, the platform provider must ensure secure and easy access. On the other hand, society generally, and particularly the young people, are used to working with mobile devices and are constantly connected with the internet. For this reason, it is an important competitive advantage that the new platform has a web-based architecture that can be accessed via the internet with any mobile device. It is also important that the platform provider creates an app with all the key functions. This ensures a real time and quick communication between the crowd and the SME for timely feedback.

6.1.6 Technology Foresight

The basic function of a crowdsourcing platform is to match the innovating companies with crowdworkers and facilitate their cooperative work on selected innovation projects. Nevertheless, the SMEs may have in their individual innovation project certain requirements or issues with which the crowd on the platform may not be able to assist. This can be the case, for example, when an innovating company has to decide between two technological solutions. However, if the innovating SME does not know if one of the two technology approaches will have future market success, technology foresight can show which technology is viable and which benefits that SME can derive from this technology (Gausemeier & Plass, 2014). When SMEs are already in contact with the platform provider, the provider may be able to offer further services in the extended innovation environment for SMEs, beyond what the crowd can provide. The SMEs can access these additional services as and when needed. This also provides the new platform with better competitive advantage in the market.

The SMEs operate in a market environment where they must be innovative to maintain their market position and to achieve growth. However, for some SMEs it could be difficult to figure out what new products or services customers would need in the coming years. At the same time, it is well known that many SMEs do not know-how to perform an innovation project in a structured manner. To meet this need of SMEs, the new platform should offer an additional technology scouting and technology foresight service. By using such a service based on their individual needs, some SMEs may be able to conceive more effective innovation projects as well as being able to execute them more efficiently.

6.1.7 Innovation Process Consulting

Furthermore, as both the interviews and the survey have shown, German manufacturing SMEs do not have a structured innovation process. Since a process modification or the introduction of new processes is very difficult for SMEs because for this, different stakeholders have to be very involved in the process at a very early stage, it makes sense that the platform provider also offers a need-based innovation process consultancy. The SMEs can then operate both the traditional crowdsourcing and the use of corresponding additional services made available by the platform provider.

6.1.8 Matchmaking Area

Both the interviews and survey conducted as a part of this research show that the responding SMEs cooperate with other companies and research facilities to carry out their R&D projects. These partners are invariably found by the innovating SME from within their close business environment. This, however, does not always happen. In some cases, the SMEs find it difficult to find and engage with a suitable innovation partner. In some cases, an innovation network can assist them. However, desired innovation success may not be achieved due to a mismatch between SMEs requirements and what the potential partners in the local network can offer. For this reason, the proposed crowdsourcing platform should support the innovating SMEs to find suitable innovation partners when needed. In an online matchmaking space various SMEs, research institutes and universities can be listed, and their abilities can be showcased. Furthermore, they can also explicitly express the terms of their willingness for a possible R&D cooperation.

6.1.9 Financial Support by Government-Granted Subsidized Funds

The financing of innovation is crucial for SMEs. In most cases, the SMEs reinvest their own profits in their innovation. In addition, government subsidies made available to SMEs are also used to finance R&D projects. Unfortunately, the survey has confirmed the personal experience of the author, that these government R&D subsidies were not designed optimally for the SMEs. In this area, a distinction has to be made between so-called cooperation projects and solo projects. In both areas, a two-stage application procedure is used in many programmes. This means that the innovating project partners must first submit a project outline to a project promoter. This project promoter examines the degree of innovation, the financial situation of the applicant SME, and the ability of the SME to innovate in the sense of the project application and the corresponding innovation risk. If the innovating project partners have successfully passed this first step, they will need to submit a detailed R&D project application to the promoter in the second step to apply for funding for this project. These applications must be prepared in great detail by each project partner. This requires considerable time, human resources and organizational effort from SMEs. Furthermore, the project documentation as well as the corresponding project section reports must be submitted to the promoter during the year. This also causes considerable expense for SMEs. Given the magnitude of these efforts, it is not surprising that the surveyed companies are very reluctant to use such subsidy programmes, because the bureaucratic burden of applying is much too high for an SME. Therefore, the new platform should offer a further service through which the necessary administrative work in a government-funded R&D project is carried out by the specialists of the platform in consultation with the innovating SMEs. This means that the SMEs only have a minimum application cost, with most of the effort being made by the platform staff. This additional service differentiates the new platform from other existing platforms and adds value to the link between the innovating SMEs and the platform.

6.1.10 Intellectual Property Rights Trading Area

As also identified in the surveys, SMEs want to commercialize the individual innovation outcomes. This is usually achieved by creating new products or services, or by making innovative modifications to existing products. However, if an SME cannot readily integrate the R&D outcomes into existing products or cannot commercialize it in new products, SMEs should still be able to benefit from its R&D activities and innovation projects in another manner. They can do this either by selling the innovation results, as an intellectual property right, or by making the innovation results available to several different interested parties through licensing. For this reason, the new platform also offers an IP trading area where SMEs can offer the outcomes of its innovation projects for use or for sale.

6.1.11 Invoicing Model

Financial resources are always crucial for businesses, particularly SMEs. Therefore, the invoicing model of the new platform is of particular importance for its success or failure. SMEs need a well-calculated budget, with no hidden costs or additional costs incurred during the use of the platform. Furthermore, the SMEs need a low-threshold offer, so that the use of the platform does not exceed the innovation project budget of the SME. For this reason, it makes sense to cover the basic costs including a profit margin for the basic services of the platform plus an additional small monthly charge, like that in a subscription model. The basic services in the context of a crowdsourcing platform are the traditional crowdsourcing processes which SMEs can independently carry out via the platform. These basic services must be fully automated via the platform so that no further innovation specialist has to be taken care of for the basic functions. The additional services described above are also offered depending on the intensity of use or on a fixed charge. The invoicing modalities must be agreed in advance individually between the SMEs and the platform provider.

Crowdsourcing is a suitable way to support the SMEs in their innovation. This lays the foundations of a feasible innovation infrastructure. However, to take advantage of this infrastructure, it is necessary that SMEs in turn establish sound innovation management practices. This means that innovating companies that want to access the crowdsourcing infrastructure need to invest resources and build appropriate capabilities. It can be emphasized that, according to this study, there is need for a crowdsourcing platform with the above-identified plug-ins to be set up for German SMEs. However, there are some prerequisites for it to happen. On the one hand, the new platform provider must have the technical know-how to facilitate necessary technical features on the online platform. If the new provider does not have the relevant know-how, it may make it possible by appropriate arrangement with some external development service provider. Furthermore, to provide the extended service features suggested above the new platform provider will need further engagement with the specialists for technology scouting, IP trading, innovation process consulting and technology consulting, as well as with other agencies with expertise in dealing with the application process of the government support R&D programmes for innovative companies.

References

Gausemeier, J., & Plass, C. (2014). *Zukunftsorientierte Unternehmensgestaltung: Strategien, Geschäftsprozesse und IT-Systeme für die Produktion von morgen* (2., überarb. Aufl). Hanser.

Vyas, V. (2005). Imitation, incremental innovation and climb down: A strategy for survival and growth of new ventures. *The Journal of Entrepreneurship, 14*(2), 103–116. https://doi.org/10.1177/097135570501400202

Appendices

A.1 Measurement Framework of the European Innovation Scoreboard

See Table A.1.

A.2 The European Innovation Performance Index

See Table A.2.

A.3 Overview of Internal and External Financing Options for Innovations

See Table A.3.

A.4 Types of Crowdsourcing Platforms

See Tables A.4, A.5, A.6, A.7, and A.8.

M. Vathauer, *Breaking Barriers with Open Innovation in Germany*, Management for Professionals, https://doi.org/10.1007/978-3-032-14660-1

Table A.1 Measurement framework of the European Innovation Scoreboard

Item number	Measurement framework	Measured items
1	Human resources	New doctorate graduates
2		Population aged 25–34 with tertiary education
3		Lifelong learning
4	Attractive research systems	International scientific co-publications
5		Top 10% most cited publications
6		Foreign doctorate students
7	Innovation-friendly environment	Broadband penetration
8		Opportunity-driven entrepreneurship
9	Finance and support	R&D expenditure in the public sector
10		Venture capital expenditures
11	Firm investments	R&D expenditure in the business sector
12		Non-R&D innovation expenditures
13		Enterprises providing training to develop or upgrade ICT skills of their personnel
14	Innovators	SMEs with product or process innovations
15		SMEs with marketing or organizational innovations
16		SMEs innovating in-house
17	Linkages	Innovative SMEs collaborating with others
18		Public–private co-publications
19		Private co-funding of public R&D expenditures
20	Intellectual assets	PCT patent applications
21		Trademark applications
22		Design applications
23	Employment impacts	Employment in knowledge-intensive activities
24		Employment fast-growing enterprises of innovative sectors
25	Sales impacts	Medium and high-tech product exports
26		Knowledge-intensive services exports
27		Sales of new-to-market and new-to-firm product innovations

Source European Commission (2018, p. 8)

Table A.2 Innovation performance groups; own illustration

Performance groups	Result
Innovation leaders	· Innovation performance is well above that of the EU. More than 20% above the EU average · Denmark, Finland, The Netherlands and Sweden
Strong innovators	· Member States with a performance close to that of the EU average, but less than 20% above or more than 90% of the EU average · Belgium, Germany, Austria, France, Ireland, Luxembourg, Cyprus, Estonia
Moderate innovators	· Member States where the innovation performance is below that of the EU average at relative performance rates between 50 and 90% of the EU average · Slovenia, Czech Republic, Greece, Hungary, Italy, Lithuania, Malta, Portugal and Spain
Modest innovator	· Modest innovators include Member States that show an innovation performance level well below that of the EU average, less than 50% of the EU average · Poland, Bulgaria, Latvia, Romania, Croatia and Slovakia

Source European Commission (2018, p. 7)

Table A.3 Overview of internal and external financing options

No	Funding opportunity	Notes
1	Reinvesting profits	Internal sources
2	New capital	Internal sources
3	Bank loans	External sources
4	Other dept contracts	External sources
5	Government grants	External public sources
6	Tax credits	External public sources
7	Crowd funding	External public sources
8	Venture Capital	External venture sources

Source Belitz and Lejpras (2014, pp. 4–6)

Table A.4 Research- and Development platforms intermediary platforms

Type of intermediary platform	Name of intermediary platform	Web address	Application	Country	Language
Research- and Development platforms	InnoCentive	www.innocentive.com	Problem solving scientific-based questions	USA	English
	TekScout	N.A.	Problem solving scientific-based questions	N.A.	N.A.
	IdeaConnection	www.ideaconnection.com	Idea creation platform	Canada	English
	Yet2.com	www.yet2.com	Trade platform for copyrights	USA, UK, Japan	English, Japanese
	PRESANS	www.presans.com	Problem solving scientific-based questions	France	English
	Hypios	www.hypios-ci.com	Problem solving scientific-based questions	France	French
	NineSigma	www.ninesigma.com	Platform for solving technical issues	Japan, Belgium, USA	English
	Pharma Licensing	www.pharmaLicensing.com	Platform for Technology Scouting, Technology Marketing and Government & Education which is related to the pharmaceutical industry	USA, UK	English

Source Gassmann (2010)

Table A.5 Marketing and Design Platforms intermediary platforms

Type of intermediary platform	Name of intermediary platform	Web address	Application	Country	Language
Marketing and design platforms	RedesignMe	www.redesignme.com	Logo design and corporate design	The Netherlands, USA	English
	Idea Bounty	https://www.ideaconnection.com/outsourcing/idea-bounty-23.html	Marketing competitions, marketing activities	N.A.	English
	crowdSPRING	www.crowdspring.com	Logo design and corporate design	USA	English
	Battle of concepts	https://www.battleofconcepts.nl	Innovation concepts can be challenged by the crowd	The Netherlands	Dutch / English
	Brand Tags	N.A.	Platform to share knowledge and experiences about markets	N.A.	N.A.
	Guerra Creativa	https://www.guerra-creativa.com/en/	Crowdsourcing platform for logos, websites and more	Argentina	Spanish, Portuguese, English
	99designs	https://99designs.de/	Platform for Logo-Design, Website-Design, Print-Design, T-Shirt Print-Design	Germany	German

(continued)

Table A.5 (continued)

Type of intermediary platform	Name of intermediary platform	Web address	Application	Country	Language
	12designer	Was taken over by 99designs	Platform for Logo-Design, Flyer-Design, Website-Design		
	Logo Arena	https://www.logoarena.de/	Platform for a company-logo competition by 50 or more suggestion which created the individual company logo	Canada	German, English

Source Gassmann (2010)

Table A.6 Platforms for freelancer intermediary platforms

Type of intermediary platform	Name of intermediary platform	Web address	Application	Country	Language
Platforms for freelancer	Amazon Mechanical Turk	www.mturk.com	Simple activities	USA	English
	Spudaroo	https://www.crunchbase.com/organisation/spudaroo-com	Virtual advertising copywriter	Canada	English
	HumanGrid	Belongs to CLICKWORKER	Minor online-activities	N.A.	N.A.
	TopCoder	https://www.topcoder.com/	Crowdsourcing platform for Design &P prototyping of technical products, Software-Application development, Development of Algorithms & Analytics	USA	English
	LeadVine	https://www.leadvine.com/	'LeadVine' is an online social community that simplifies how companies find new customers. Search listings and make money with the information that you already have"	N.A.	N.A.
	AppJobber	https://www.appjobber.de/	AppJobber is a crowdsourcing platform for fast and cost-effective data collection in retail and other business-relevant locations	Germany	German, English, Spanish, French, Italian, Polish, Portuguese, Turkish
	Clickworker	https://www.clickworker.de/	Small online tasks such as web research, surveys, keywording etc	Germany	German, English
	cash4feedback	N.A.	N.A.	N.A.	N.A.
	Freelancer.com	www.freelancer.com	'Outsource anything you can think of!'	Australia	English,

Source Gassmann (2010)

Table A.7 Idea creation platforms intermediary platforms

Type of intermediary platform	Name of intermediary platform	Web address	Application	Country	Language
Idea creation platforms	Atiso	www.atiso.com	Crowdsourcing with its own innovation community	Switzerland	German
	Big Idea Group	http://www.thinkbigideagroup.com/	Innovators for ideas, marketing and products	USA	English
	Exnovate	https://www.exnovate.org/	Open innovation in a network	Belgium	English
	Chaordix	www.chaordix.com	Chaordix is a global leader in collaborative innovation and they are working with brands. As early adopters of crowdsourcing technology, the proven ability to build collaborative communities, combined with the proprietary software and methodology	Canada	English
	Innovation Exchange	http://www.ixa.nl/en/home.html	Platform for collaborative research, Science Incubator, Licensing and collaboration opportunities	The Netherlands	English

(continued)

Table A.7 (continued)

Type of intermediary platform	Name of intermediary platform	Web address	Application	Country	Language
	Idea Crossing	http://www.innovationsmethoden.info/experten/idea-crossing-inc	Idea Crossing specializes in organizing ideas competitions and innovation contests for its customers with the help of the "Challenge Accelerator" software tool	USA	English
	Jovoto	www.jovoto.com	Mass collaboration on the Jovoto platform leads to fresh ideas, from product design and marketing campaigns to innovative business scenarios of the future	Germany	English
	crowdINNO	N.A.	Platform on which competitions for innovations can be advertised	N.A.	N.A.
	Innovationskraftwerk	www.innovationskraftwerk.de	Open Innovation Platform, which not only deals with innovation and problem-solving processes in business but also scientific and socio-political issues	Germany	German, English

Source Gassmann (2010)

Table A.8 German-based crowdsourcing platforms

Category	Name of intermediary platform	Web address	Application	Location	Language
Micro-task platform	1. Clickworker 2. Mylittlejob	1. www.clickworker.com 2. www.mylittlejob.com	1. Small online tasks such as web research, surveys, keywording etc 2. Small tasks such as transcriptions, text writing, translations	Germany	German
Marketplace platform	1. Crowd Guru 2. Content.de	1. www.crowdguru.de 2. www.Content.de	1. Small tasks such as content for online-shops, website construction, text writing 2. Text writing for SEOs, blogger, online-shops, translations	Germany	German
Design platform	1. 12designer 2. designenlassen.de	1. Was taken over by 99designs 2. www.designenlassen.de	Platform for Logo-Design, Flyer-Design, Website-Design 2. Logo design, Web-design, Flyer-design	Germany	German
Testing platform	1. Applause 2. Testbirds	1. www.applause.com 2. www.testbirds.com	1. Crowd Testing, Automated testing, payment testing, accessibility testing 2. Testing of websites, testing of wearables, testing of mobile apps, testing of games	Germany	German
Innovation platforms	1. Jovoto 2. UnserAller	1. www.jovoto.com 2. www.crowdcommunity.de	Mass collaboration on the Jovoto platform leads to fresh ideas, from product design and marketing campaigns to innovative business scenarios of the future	Germany	German

Source Leimeister et al. (2016, pp. 18–19)

References

Belitz, H., & Lejpras, A. (Eds.) (2014). *Financing patterns of innovative SMEs and the perception of innovation barriers in Germany* [Special issue]. DIW Berlin, German Institute for Economic Research, 2014.

European Commission. (2014). *Innovation Union Scoreboard 2014.*

European Commission. (2018). *European Innovation Scoreboard 2018. European Innovation Scoreboard 2018.* Publications Office.

European Commission. (2024). *European Innovation Scoreboard 2024.*

Gassmann, O. (2010). *Crowdsourcing: Innovations management mit Schwarmintelligenz.* Carl Hanser Verlag GmbH & Co. KG. https://doi.org/10.3139/9783446426498

Glöckner, L. (2024). *Die problematische Lieferkette von Anwendungen Künstlicher Intelligenz.* Retrieved from https://www.recyclist-magazin.de/post/lieferkette-von-kuenstlicher-intelligenz

Healthly.AI Data, L. (2022). *Crowd workers for data collection—An indispensable part of Ethical AI.* Retrieved from http://shaip.com/blog/crowd-workers-for-data-collection-an-indispensable-part-of-responsible-ai/

Leimeister, J. M., Durward, D., & Zogaj, S. (2016). *Crowd worker in Deutschland: Eine empirische Studie zum Arbeitsumfeld auf externen Crowdsourcing-Plattformen.* Study/Hans-Böckler-Stiftung: Nr. 323. Hans-Böckler-Stiftung.

Portulans Institute (Ed.). (2024). *Network Readiness Index 2024.* Retrieved from https://networkreadinessindex.org/

Rubach, S., Johansen, F. R., & Andersson, G. (2014). Missing Actions in Cluster Innovation. *International Journal of Advanced Corporate Learning (iJAC), 7*(1), 17. https://doi.org/10.3991/ijac.v7i1.3524

Statista GmbH. (2013). *Anzahl der aktiven Crowdfunding-Plattformen* weltweit von 2010 bis 2012.* Retrieved from https://de.statista.com/statistik/daten/studie/258185/umfrage/anzahl-der-crowdfunding-plattformen-weltweit/

Statista GmbH. (2025). *Unternehmen in Deutschland: Anzahl der rechtlichen Einheiten[1] nach Rechtsform und Anzahl der Beschäftigten im Jahr 2023.* Retrieved from https://de.statista.com/statistik/daten/studie/237346/umfrage/unternehmen-in-deutschland-nach-rechtsform-und-anzahl-der-beschaeftigten/

Statistisches Bundesamt. (2025). *Mehr Unternehmensinsolvenzen im 1. Halbjahr 2025 als im 1. Halbjahr 2024.* Retrieved from https://www.destatis.de/DE/Presse/Pressemitteilungen/2025/09/PD25_332_52411.html#:~:text=12%20009%20beantragte%20Unternehmensinsolvenzen

Trott, P., & Hartmann, D. (2009). Why 'Open Innovation' is old wine in new bottles. *International Journal of Innovation Management, 13*(4), 715–736.

Yi, J., Yang, S., Yue, L., & Lei, I. M. (2025). Digital light processing 3D printing of flexible devices: Actuators, sensors and energy devices. *Microsystems & Nanoengineering, 11*(1), 51. https://doi.org/10.1038/s41378-025-00885-8

M. Vathauer, *Breaking Barriers with Open Innovation in Germany*, Management for Professionals, https://doi.org/10.1007/978-3-032-14660-1

MIX
Papier aus verantwortungsvollen Quellen
Paper from responsible sources
FSC® C105338

If you have any concerns about our products,
you can contact us on
ProductSafety@springernature.com

In case Publisher is established outside the EU,
the EU authorized representative is:
Springer Nature Customer Service Center GmbH
Europaplatz 3, 69115 Heidelberg, Germany

Printed by Libri Plureos GmbH
in Hamburg, Germany